BULIMIA

BULIMIA

A Program for Friends and Family Members

By

SANDRA KAPOOR, Ph.D., M.P.H., R.D.

Assistant Professor
School of Hotel, Restaurant and Institutional Management
Michigan State University
East Lansing, Michigan

CHARLES C THOMAS • PUBLISHER
Springfield • Illinois • U.S.A.

Published and Distributed Throughout the World by

CHARLES C THOMAS • PUBLISHER

2600 South First Street

Springfield, Illinois 62794-9265

© *1988 by* CHARLES C THOMAS • PUBLISHER

ISBN 0-398-05444-4

Library of Congress Catalog Card Number: 87-33576

With THOMAS BOOKS *careful attention is given to all details of manufacturing and*
design. It is the Publisher's desire to present books that are satisfactory as to their physical
qualities and artistic possibilities and appropriate for their particular use. THOMAS
BOOKS *will be true to those laws of quality that assure a good name and good will.*

Printed in the United States of America

Q-R-3

Library of Congress Cataloging in Publication Data

Kapoor, Sandra.
    Bulimia : a program for friends and family members.

    Bibliography: p.
    Includes index.
    1. Bulimia--Patients--Rehabilitation. I. Title.
[DNLM: 1. Bulimia--therapy. WM 175 K17b]
RC552.B84K36   1988   616.85′2   87-33576
ISBN 0-398-05444-4

This book is dedicated to all the victims of eating disorders who are struggling to recover and their concerned others who are trying to support them and manage their own bulimia-related problems that they may win their battles.

PREFACE

THE "Helping the Bulimic Get Better" program was created to assist
friends and family members of a bulimic manage bulimia-related
problems and support their bulimic's recovery. This book was written to
share this program with professionals interested in helping the concerned others of bulimics. The program is presented in the form of five
lesson plans with five optional lesson plans. Detailed instructions are
provided for implementing each of the lesson plans. Four instruments, a
knowledge test, an attitude survey, a skill device, and an evaluation form
are included to evaluate the effects of the program. The development of
the "Helping the Bulimic Get Better" program, the effects of the program on the concerned others of bulimics, and making the program a
success are also discussed.

ACKNOWLEDGMENTS

ONE EVENING my husband, Tarun, made an observation about bulimics and the people in their lives. He said,

> Bulimics can get help and support for their eating disorder. They can go to a counselor, therapist or psychiatrist; join a support group or participate in a treatment program. But what about the husband or wife, mother or father, brother or sister, or friend of the bulimic. Where can they go for help?

It was his observation that inspired the development of the "Helping the Bulimic Get Better" program, the subject of this book. For this, I am thankful to Tarun. I am thankful to him too for the support and love he gave me while I was writing this book.

I am also grateful to my three sisters, Susan, Janet, and Ellen, for always being there when I needed someone to discuss my work with, and to my advisor, Dr. Ruth Thomas for her guidance in the construction, implementation, and evaluation of the "Helping the Bulimic Get Better" program.

Three other individuals I am thankful to are the secretaries of my School at Michigan State University, Freida, Gail, and Diane. I am most appreciative to them for all their work in preparing this book.

There are many others who have contributed to this project. I am greatly indebted to all the bulimics, their friends, and family members, and the many professionals in the various disciplines who made this book possible by their generous gifts of time and/or expertise.

CONTENTS

BULIMIA

Chapter I

DEVELOPING
A BULIMIA ASSISTANCE PROGRAM

BULIMIA'S INCIDENCE

BULIMIA is a common and widespread problem. Craig Johnson, director of an eating disorder treatment program at Michael Reese Hospital in Chicago, estimates that 15 to 20 percent of America's college women have "some involvement" with binge eating and purging (Squire, 1981). The National Association of Anorexia Nervosa and Associated Disorders (ANAD) estimates its incidence is even greater (Neuman & Halvorson, 1983). They estimate between 20 and 30 percent of college women engage in bulimic behavior.

BULIMIA'S EFFECTS

If not recognized and treated, bulimia can lead to lifelong physical and emotional problems. The medical complications (University California, Los Angeles Eating Disorders Clinic, personal communication, January 25, 1984) may involve the following:

1. chronic esophagitis
2. esophageal rupture
3. gastric dilation
4. gastric rupture
5. electrolyte imbalance
6. abuse of ipecac syrup, an emetic, has caused emetine cardiomyopathy and irreversible congestive failure leading to death in several patients reported in the literature

3

7. chronic parotid gland enlargement
8. electrolyte abnormalities, especially hypokalemic metabolic al-
   kalosis that can lead to cardiac arrhythmias
9. volume dehydration
10. rectal prolapse and/or megacolon
11. irritable bowel syndrome
12. chronic edema
13. dental erosion
14. diaphragmatic rupture with entrance of the abdominal contents
    into the chest cavity
15. amenorrhea

For many, the emotional effects of the eating disorder (Anorexia
Nervosa & Related Eating Disorders, Inc. [ANRED], personal communication, January 15, 1984) are worse than the physical complications. An overwhelming amount of guilt, depression, misery, and
confusion often accompanies the eating disorder. For some, this leads to
agonizing feelings of hopelessness and despair.

BULIMIA'S OTHER VICTIMS

Bulimics are not the only victims of this disorder. Their close friends
and family members are its victims, too. Since these significant others
are usually intimately involved in the eating problem, they are seriously
affected by it as well (Boskind-White & White, 1983; Cauwels, 1983;
Kinoy, Miller, Atchley & Book Committee of the American Anorexia/
Bulimia Association, 1984). While bulimics suffer from bulimia's physical and psychological complications, their friends and relatives suffer
from not being able to cope with the frustration and anguish which results from bulimic behavior.

Even as concerned others are experiencing their own problems from
being involved with a bulimic, it is essential for them to be supportive of
their bulimic's recovery. This was found to be the case in a study
(Boskind-White & White, 1983) conducted at Cornell University in
1974. It involved twenty-six women struggling with bulimia who participated in a pilot therapy program. Although some did well initially, they
were consistently unable to sustain their progress. A follow-up question-
naire revealed 96 percent reverted to their former eating patterns within
two months after treatment. Their failure was attributed to lack of criti-
cal sources of support upon leaving therapy.

Generally, friends and family members want to support their bulimic's strides towards recovery. They just don't know how (Cauwels, 1983).

Recovery is not easy for either party. Each is faced with the task of dealing with the bulimia. Even as the friends and relatives are attempting to manage their own problems produced by the bulimia, though, their bulimics need them to be supportive of their recovery. Significant others' failure to do so may deter their bulimic's progress in recovery.

PROGRAMS FOR FRIENDS AND FAMILIES

Currently, it appears little information pertaining to programs for friends and family members of bulimics has been published. However, investigations have shown that when friends and family members of alcoholics participated in a program designed for them, they as well as their alcoholic benefited (Cork, 1956; Gliedman, Rosenthal, Frank & Nash, 1956; Igersheimer, 1959; McDowell, 1972; Smith, 1969). The similar personality and behavior characteristics of bulimics and alcoholics (Hatsukami, Owen, Pyle & Mitchell, 1982; Johnson & Berndt, 1983) suggest a program for friends and family members of bulimics could likewise benefit both parties.

Given the current seriousness and prevalence of bulimia, the effect it is having on the significant others of those with bulimia, the ability of significant others to be a valuable source of support to the bulimic's recovery and the potential benefits of a program for both bulimics and their friends and family members, "Helping the Bulimic Get Better" program was developed. It was designed to help significant others (1) support their bulimic's recovery and (2) resolve the dilemmas produced by being involved with a bulimic.

BASIS FOR PROGRAM DEVELOPMENT

The program was developed on the basis of findings from a review of three areas of literature and through interviews with bulimics, their concerned others and eating disorder specialists. Based on the problems friends and relatives described in the literature and the interviews, the aims, educational objectives, learner outcomes and content for the "Helping the Bulimic Get Better" program were constructed. The curriculum, the educational materials and the instructional format for the program were developed from three models of teaching. They were the transmitter of knowledge model (Sprinthall & Sprinthall, 1981), the role-playing model (Shaftel & Shaftel, 1976, 1982), and the classroom meeting model (Joyce & Weil, 1978). Findings from the alcohol literature also guided the development of the "Helping the Bulimic Get Better" program. Direction was obtained from the alcohol literature on: how to administer a program for concerned others, how to get concerned others to register for a program, how to keep concerned others attending a program for them, what information concerned others need about bulimia, and what educational approaches are most appropriate for treating concerned others. An in depth review of the literature is provided in "Effects of an Educational Intervention on the Significant Others of Bulimics" (Kapoor, 1986).

PROGRAM FEATURES

The "Helping the Bulimic Get Better" program is a five-week program with one-and-one-half-hour meetings scheduled once a week. Its purpose is to help the relatives and friends of a practicing or recovering bulimic to (1) learn more about how to assist their bulimic get better and (2) learn to deal with the problems produced by being involved with a bulimic.

One problem is addressed at each session of the program. The problems are:

1. Understanding what bulimia is, its causes and incidence.
2. Knowing what the effects of bulimia are and its treatment.
3. Coping with food situations involving the bulimic.
4. Dealing with the bulimic's failure to be abstinent.
5. Helping the bulimic be abstinent.

The program may be expanded to address other problems faced by friends and families of bulimics. They are:

1. Stop blaming themselves or others for a loved one's eating disorder.
2. Developing trust in one's bulimic.
3. Managing negative feelings produced by being involved with a bulimic.
4. Knowing what healthy eating is and how to implement a healthy eating plan for themselves.

Information sharing is the primary activity in the first two sessions. During these two sessions group members are also provided opportunities to get to know and become comfortable with one another. These two sessions set the stage for group members to examine problems and discuss methods for dealing with these problems in later sessions.

Each session follows this format:

1. *Immediate concerns.* During this period, program participants have the opportunity to share immediate concerns regarding the bulimic in their life. Each session opens with ten to fifteen minutes for sharing these pressing problems. Immediate concerns can be related to anything. Discussing them immediately frees members of the group to concentrate later when the session's assigned topic is presented. It is also a time when concerned others can get support and insight from other group members on how to manage the challenges of being involved with a bulimic.

2. *Discussion of home assignment.* In this activity, group members talk about the tasks they have been assigned to work on at home. This helps them to take responsibility for their own learning. It also enables them to be acknowledged for their efforts and reinforced for their successes. It is the facilitator's responsibility to communicate an expectation that home assignments will be done.

3. *Presentation of content.* At each session, one problem produced by being involved with a bulimic is addressed. Methods employed are lectures, movies, handouts, role-playing, overheads, discussions, case studies, and home assignments.

4. *Application of content.* At this time, group members are encouraged to question the content of the session and examine how it relates to their own situation. It is preferred that group members discover their own personal applications rather than having them directly applied for them. The role of the facilitator is to be aware of the various issues involved and to give ideas to stimulate the discussion.

5. *Home assignments.* Through assignments to do at home, concerned others are able to make the content of each session relevant in their lives. In the assignments they are asked to examine how they manage problems involving their bulimic and support their bulimic's recovery from the eating disorder. Assignment sheets are provided outlining the tasks to be performed each week.

The program facilitator may also choose to schedule an individual meeting with each concerned other prior to the first group meeting. At this time the program facilitator can explain the program, obtain the concerned other's commitment to attend all five sessions (see Form I), and conduct any preprogram testing desired. A bulimia knowledge, bulimia attitude, and bulimia skill test are provided in Chapter VI. They measure the effects of the "Helping the Bulimic Get Better" program. Measures of reliability and validity were calculated for each of these instruments.

The individual meeting further allows friends and family members to address concerns or questions they have about the program. It is an opportunity for the facilitator to ease any fears significant others have about attending the "Helping the Bulimic Get Better" program.

The program facilitator may also schedule an individual or group meeting following the last session of the program. At this meeting, post-testing and an evaluation (see Chapter VI) of the program can be conducted. If post testing is to be conducted with the bulimia skill instrument, individual meetings with significant others will be required. Otherwise, a group meeting will suffice.

FORM I
ATTENDANCE COMMITMENT

I agree to attend all *five* meetings of the "Helping the Bulimic Get Better" program (and one follow-up meeting after the program is finished). I will complete the required home assignments and make every effort to participate in the program. If an emergency prevents me from attending a meeting, I will contact the group facilitator prior to the meeting.

Significant Other: _____   Date: _____

Group Facilitator: _____   Date: _____

Chapter II

IMPLEMENTING A BULIMIA ASSISTANCE PROGRAM — PART ONE

THIS chapter contains the lesson plans for the five sessions of the "Helping the Bulimic Get Better" program. They are:

- Understanding What Bulimia Is
- More About Bulimia
- Coping with Food Situations Involving the Bulimic
- Dealing with the Bulimic's Failure to be Abstinent
- Helping the Bulimic be Abstinent

UNDERSTANDING WHAT BULIMIA IS

Instructional Objectives

This session is designed to help significant others to:

1. meet other friends and family members who are unable to manage the problems produced by being involved with a bulimic.
2. become knowledgeable about what bulimia is, its causes and incidence.

Learner Outcomes

After completing this session, significant others should be able to:

1. define bulimia.
2. outline the criteria used to diagnose bulimia.
3. describe bulimia's victims.
4. identify possible causes of bulimia.

Activities

Facilitator	—welcomes program participants
	—gives out name tags
	—introduces self
	—describes experiences with bulimia
Group members	—introduce themselves
	—describe experiences with bulimia
Facilitator	—discusses five-week program schedule
	—indicates importance of maintaining anonymity
	—explains the format each session will follow
	—passes out handouts
	—introduces lecture on bulimia
	—provides information about bulimia's definition, causes and incidence
	—summarizes session's happenings
	—gives home assignment
	—describes upcoming week's topic

Handout Materials

Program Schedule
Bulimia Outline
Book List

Articles from Popular Magazines List
Homework
Name Tags

Visual Aids

Bulimia Outline Overhead
Bulimia Criteria Overhead

Equipment

Overhead Projector
Chalkboard

References

American Psychiatric Association. (1980). *Diagnostic and statistical manual of mental disorders* (3rd ed.). Washington, DC: Author.

Boskind-Lodhal, M. (1976). Cinderella's stepsister: A feminist perspective on anorexia nervosa and bulimia. *Signs: Journal of Women in Culture and Society, 2,* 342-356.

Boskind-White, M., & White, W.C., Jr. (1983). *Bulimarexia the binge/purge cycle.* New York: W. W. Norton.

Bruch, H. (1973). *Eating disorders.* New York: Basic Books.

Casper, R.C., Eckert, E.D., Halmi, K.A. (1980). Bulimia: Its incidence and clinical importance in patients with anorexia nervosa. *Archives of General Psychiatry, 37,* 1030-1035.

Cauwels, J.M. (1983). *Bulimia the binge-purge compulsion.* New York: Doubleday.

Fairburn, C. (1981). A cognitive behavioral approach to the treatment of bulimia. *Psychological Medicine,* 11, 707-711.

Fischel, A. (Producer & Director). (1982). *I don't have to hide.* [Film]. Jamaica Plains, NY: Fanlight Productions.

Goff, G.M. (1984). *Bulimia: The binge-eating and purging syndrome.* Center City, MN: Hazelden.

Green, R.J., & Rau, J.H. (1974). Treatment of compulsive eating disturbances with anticonvulsant medication. *American Journal of Psychiatry, 131,* 428-432.

Halmi, K.A. (1983). Anorexia nervosa and bulimia. *Psychosomatics, 24,* 111-129.

Halmi, K.A., Falk, J.R., & Schwartz, E. (1981). Binge-eating and vomiting: A survey of a college population. *Psychological Medicine, 11,* 697-706.

Hawkins, R.C., Freemouw, W.J. & Clement, P.F. (1984). *The binge-purge syndrome.* New York: Springer.

Herzog, D.B. (1982). Bulimia: The secretive syndrome. *Psychosomatics,* 23: 481-487.

Johnson, C.L. & Larson, R. (1982). Bulimia: An analysis of moods and behavior. *Psychosomatic Medicine,* 44, 333-345.

Kinoy, B.P., Miller, E.B., Atchley, J.A., & Book Committee of the American Anorexia/Bulimia Association. (1984). *When will we laugh again?* New York: Columbia University Press.

Loro, A.D., & Orleans, C.S. (1981). Binge eating in obesity: Preliminary findings and guidelines for behavioral analysis and treatment. *Addictive Behaviors, 6,* 155-166.

Mitchell, J.E., & Pyle, R.L. (1981). The bulimic syndrome in normal weight individuals: A review. *International Journal of Eating Disorders, 1* (2), 61-73.

Neuman, P.A. & Halvorson, P.A. (1983). *Anorexia nervosa and bulimia.* New York: Van Nostrand-Reinhold.

Pyle, R.L., Mitchell, J.E., & Eckert, E.D. (1981). Bulimia: A report of 34 cases. *Journal of Clinical Psychiatry, 42,* 60-64.

Rosen, J.C., & Leitenberg, H. (1982). Treatment with exposure and response prevention. *Behavior Therapy, 13,* 117-124.

Russell, G. (1979). Bulimia nervosa: An ominous variant of anorexia nervosa. *Psychological Medicine, 9,* 429-448.

Sprinthall, R.C., & Sprinthall, N.A. (1981). *Educational psychology: A developmental approach* (3rd ed.) Reading, MA: Addison-Wesley.

Squire, S. (1981, October). Why thousands of women don't know how to eat normally anymore. *Glamour,* pp. 245, 309-311.

Walsh, B.T., Stewart, J.W., Wright, L., Marrison, W., Rosse, S.P., & Glassman, A.H. (1982). Treatment of bulimia with monoamine oxidase inhibitors. *American Journal of Psychiatry, 139,* 1629-1630.

Wardle, J. (1980). Dietary restraint and binge eating. *Behavioral Analysis and Modification, 4,* 201-209.

Wardle, J., & Beinart, H. (1981). Binge eating: A theoretical review. *British Journal of Social and Clinical Psychology, 20,* 97-109.

Bulimia Outline

I. Definition of bulimia
  A. Nicole's story
  B. Bulimia's other names
    1. Bulimarexia
    2. Dietary chaos syndrome
    3. Bulimia nervosa
  C. Psychiatric illness
    1. *Diagnostic and Statistical Manual of Mental Disorders,* Third Edition-Revised
    2. Diagnostic criteria
      a. Recurrent episodes of binge-eating (rapid consumption of a large amount of food in a discrete period of time, usually less than two hours)
      b. At least three of the following:
        1. Consumption of high-calorie, easily ingested food during a binge
        2. Inconspicuous eating during a binge
        3. Termination of such eating episodes by abdominal pain, sleep, social interruption or self-induced vomiting
        4. Repeated attempts to lose weight by severely restrictive diets, self-induced vomiting, or use of cathartics or diuretics
        5. Frequent weight fluctuations greater than ten pounds due to alternating binges and fasts
      c. Awareness that the eating pattern is abnormal and fear of not being able to stop eating voluntarily
      d. Depressed mood and self-deprecating thoughts following eating binges
      e. The bulimic episodes are not due to anorexia nervosa or any known physical disorder

II. Incidence of bulimia
  A. 20-30 percent college age women
  B. Incidence unclear
    1. Ashamed of illness
    2. Don't look sick
    3. Weight within normal range
    4. No one else has the problem
    5. Afraid no effective treatment

      C. Primarily in women
        1. All types
        2. Average age of onset is eighteen
III. Cause of bulimia
    A. Unknown
    B. Weight loss
    C. Diets
    D. Stressful life situations
    E. Fear of rejection
    F. Many other factors

Bulimia Lecture

Definition of Bulimia

Introduction. Many of you probably have questions about some aspect of bulimia. You may wonder, how common is the illness? What causes it? What are the physical complications that result from it and can one ultimately die from it? Tonight, we will attempt to answer these and your other questions about bulimia by providing you with some general information about the disorder.

NICOLE'S STORY[1]

Let's begin with Nicole's story.

Nicole awakes in her cold dark room and already wishes it was time to go back to bed. She dreads the thought of going through this day, which will be like so many others in her recent past. She asks herself the question every morning: "Will I be able to make it through the day without being totally obsessed by thoughts of food, or will I blow it again and spend the day binge-ing?" She tells herself that today she will begin a new life, today she will start to live like a normal human being. However, she is not at all convinced that the choice is hers.

She feels fat and wants to lose weight, so she decides to start a new diet: "This time it'll be for real! I know I'll feel good about myself if I'm thinner. I want to start my exercises again because I want to make my body more attractive."

Nicole plans her breakfast, but decides not to eat until she has worked out for a half-hour or so. She tries not to think about food since she is not really hungry. She feels anxiety about the day ahead of her. "It's this tension," she rationalizes. That is what is making her want to eat.

Nicole showers and dresses and plans her schedule for the day — classes, studying, and meals. She plans this schedule in great detail, listing where she will be at every minute and what she will eat at every meal. She does not want to leave blocks of time when she might feel tempted to binge.

"It's time to exercise, but I don't really want to; I feel lazy. Why do I always feel so lazy? What happened to the willpower I used to have?"

Gradually, Nicole feels the binge-ing signal coming on. Half-heartedly she tries to fight it, remembering the promises she made to herself about changing. She also knows how she is going to feel at the end of the day if she spends it binge-ing. Ultimately, Nicole decides to give into her urges because, for the moment, she would rather eat.

---

1. Reprinted from *Bulimarexia the Binge/Purge Cycle* by Marlene Boskind-White, Ph.D. and William C. White, Jr., Ph.D., by permission of W.W. Norton & Company, Inc. Copyright (c) 1983 by Marlene Boskind-White and William C. White, Jr.

Since Nicole is not going to exercise, because she wants to eat, she decides that she might as well eat some "good" food. She makes a poached egg and toast and brews a cup of coffee, all of which goes down in about thirty seconds. She knows this is the beginning of several hours of craziness!

After rummaging through the cupboards, Nicole realizes that she does not have any binge food. It is cold and snowy outside and she has to be at school fairly soon, but she bundles up and runs down the street. First she stops at the bakery for a bagful of sweets—cookies, and doughnuts. While munching on these, she stops and buys a few bagels. Then a quick run to the grocery store for granola and milk. At the last minute, Nicole adds several candy bars. By the time she is finished, she has spent over fifteen dollars.

Nicole can hardly believe that she is going to put all of this food, this junk, into her body; even so, her adrenaline is flowing and all she wants to do is eat, think about eating, and anticipate getting it over with. She winces at the thought of how many pounds all of this food represents, but knows she will throw it up afterward. There is no need to worry.

At home Nicole makes herself a few bowls of cereal and milk, which she gobbles down with some of the bagels smothered with butter, cream cheese, and jelly (not to mention the goodies from the bakery and the candy bars which she is still working on). She drowns all of this with huge cups of hot coffee and milk, which help speed up the process even more. All this has taken no longer than forty-five minutes, and Nicole feels as though she has been moving at ninety miles an hour.

Nicole dreads reaching this stage, where she is so full that she absolutely has to stop eating. She will throw up, which she feels she has to do but which repels her. At this point, she has to acknowledge that she's been binge-ing. She wishes she were dreaming, but knows all too well that this is real. The thought of actually digesting all of those calories, all of that junk, terrifies her.

In her bathroom, Nicole ties her hair back, turns on the shower (so none of the neighbors can hear her), drinks a big glass of water, and proceeds to force herself to vomit. She feels sick, ashamed, and incredulous that she is really doing this. Yet she feels trapped—she does not know how to break out of this pattern. As her stomach empties, she steps on and off the scale to make sure she has not gained any weight.

Nicole knows she needs help, but she wants someone else to make it all go away. As she crashes on her bed to recuperate, her head is spinning. "I'll never do this again," she vows. "Starting tomorrow, I'm going to change. I'll go on a fast for a week and then I'll feel better."

Unfortunately, deep inside, Nicole does not believe any of this. She knows this will not be the last time. Reluctantly, she leaves for school, late and unwilling to face the work and responsibilities that lie ahead.

She almost feels as though she could eat again to avoid going to school. She wonders how many hours it will be until she starts her next binge, and she wishes she had never gotten out of bed this morning.

Nicole has been a binger for five years. She started binge-ing once a week and moved to several times a day after the first year. There were very few days when she did not binge. If she refrained, it was only because of "white knuckling it" (as she put it), which she could hardly maintain for more than a day.

The binge-ing started when Nicole arrived on campus as a freshman. She gained fifteen pounds and felt alone and unable to maintain a diet. Nicole added to her isolation by choosing to live in a single room. Her binges increased in frequency and duration in her junior year, when she became engaged to a medical student and moved in with him. It was Allen who jokingly suggested one night that she force herself to vomit after one of her typical "poor me" dialogues about how much she had eaten and how awful she looked. Nicole's misery and shame increased as she grew thinner and more dependent on purging to offset her binges. Allen and Nicole lived together for one year before Nicole fled the relationship for the "safety" of her family. However, since she had traded one form of dependency for another and was doing little more than "hanging out" at her family's home, she continued to binge and vomit. At the urging of her family, she began intensive psychotherapy, but after six months of dealing exclusively with the past, Nicole felt more hopeless and locked into the behavior than ever.

Nicole suffers from bulimia, a cyclical eating disorder that has reached epidemic proportions in our culture. The details of a typical day in Nicole's life are not pleasant to read about and certainly are not pleasant to live through. Her day may differ in certain aspects from that of other bulimic women, but her behavior and her ways of coping with stress will be all too familiar to the thousands of women who alternately binge and then purge by self-induced vomiting, the abuse of laxatives and diuretics, or severe fasting.

Bulimia literally means ox hunger, a misnomer, however, since hunger has little to do with the illness. Its victims regularly gorge themselves with food, especially high calorie food like ice cream, candy bars, cookie dough, and sweet rolls. To avoid gaining weight they purge themselves after each binge. They may self-induce vomiting or abuse diuretics and laxatives. It would not be uncommon for the bulimic who abuses laxatives to take as many as three hundred per day. Some bulimics alternate their gorging with severe fasting aided by weight reducing pills containing amphetamines. Some exercise excessively.

At some point, the bulimic's concern with the weight loss loses its importance and he/she becomes hooked on the tranquilizing effect of the gorge-purging. Most bulimics eventually learn to vomit by simple reflex actions, as though it were normal. They no longer need to stick their fingers or the end of their toothbrush down their throat. They just bend over the toilet and eliminate the contents of their binge.

Bulimia's Other Names

You have probably heard this condition referred to by a variety of names. They include bulimarexia, dietary chaos syndrome, bulimia nervosa, and bulimia. Obviously, there was no point in having several names for the disorder. So in 1980 the American Psychiatric Association defined bulimia and established criteria by which a psychiatrist or psychologist could diagnose the syndrome as a psychiatric illness. These diagnostic criteria were published in the Diagnostic and Statistical Manual of Mental Disorders (American Psychiatric Association, 1980). They are the following:

Psychiatric Illness

The criteria used to establish bulimia as a psychiatric illness are outlined in the *Diagnostic and Statistical Manual of Mental Disorders,* Third Edition-Revised. These criteria are:

A. Recurrent episodes of binge-eating (rapid consumption of a large amount of food in a discrete period of time, usually less than two hours)
B. At least three of the following:
    1. Consumption of high-calorie, easily ingested food during a binge
    2. Inconspicuous eating during a binge
    3. Termination of such eating episodes by abdominal pain, sleep, social interruption, or self-induced vomiting
    4. Repeated attempts to lose weight by severely restrictive diets, self-induced vomiting, or use of cathartics or diuretics
    5. Frequent weight fluctuations greater than ten pounds due to alternating binges and fasts
C. Awareness that the eating pattern is abnormal and fear of not being able to stop eating voluntarily
D. Depressed mood and self-deprecating thoughts following eating binges
E. The bulimic episodes are not due to anorexia nervosa or any know physical disorder

A discussion of the criteria used to diagnose bulimia follows.

A. Recurrent episodes of binge-eating (rapid consumption of a large amount of food in a discrete period of time, usually less than two hours).

    A study (Goff, 1984) of victims with bulimia found the frequency of binge eating episodes varied from once a week to as many as forty-six times a week, with an average frequency of twelve times a week. Well, you may think twelve times a week, that means on the average the bulimic in this study didn't even binge twice a day. However, the average binge usually lasted slightly over an hour. Some were shorter, as little as fifteen minutes. Others were much longer. Some bulimics in this study reported binging for eight hours at a time. So if we take a bulimic who is just binging the average, twelve times a week, lasting the average of a little over an hour, say an hour and ten minutes, in every seven days she spends fourteen hours or the equivalent of the waking hours of one day binging. The bulimic who is binging more than the average say twenty or thirty times a week and spending two or three hours per binge, is literally wasting his/her life away. That's not to mention the time he/she spends thinking about food, buying food, preparing food, cleaning up his/her cooking and eating mess and purging.

The amount of food consumed in a binge varies too. In this study (Goff, 1984) binges ranged from 1,200 calories to 11,500 calories. When you stop and think, 11,500 calories is enough calories to meet the energy needs of a one-hundred-sixty pound man for four days. This explains why the expense to carry on the habit can be phenomenal.

B. At least three of the following:
  1. Consumption of high-calorie, easily ingested food during a binge.

    Ice cream and chocolate are two common binge foods. Sweet rolls, doughnuts, bars, cakes, and cookies, and the doughs and batters they are made from, are typical binge foods, as well. Bulimics will binge on lots of other foods too. Pasta dishes, like macaroni and cheese or spaghetti with tomato sauce, bread, toasted or made into a sandwich, like peanut butter or egg salad, are often binged on. Potato products are binged on frequently too. It would not be uncommon for a bulimic to include french fries, potato chips, or mashed potatoes in a binge. Vegetables and meat are seldom binge foods. It's rare for a bulimic to binge on lettuce, for example.
  2. Inconspicuous eating during a binge

    The bulimic is very careful to make sure no one finds out about his/her disgusting habit. Many bulimics live alone, so they can practice the behavior. Some bulimics binge in their cars. Those who have roommates or live at home often can't wait until their housemates go out. If a family member or roommate returns home unexpectedly to find the bulimic making cookie dough to binge on or eating a large plate of spaghetti at four o'clock in the afternoon, the bulimic will probably lie about what he/she is doing. He/she may explain the cookie dough like this, "Oh, yea, didn't I tell you, I have to bring cookies for the church bake sale." He/she may excuse the spaghetti by saying something like, "Oh, I haven't eaten a thing all day. I was just starved and couldn't wait for dinner."

3. Termination of such eating episodes by abdominal pain, sleep, social interception, or self-induced vomiting

   Bulimics may stop an eating binge because their stomachs are so full they hurt. They may stop a binge by sleeping or vomiting the contents of their binge. When someone calls or visits them, often bulimics won't answer the door or phone. They don't want to be interrupted while they are binging.

4. Repeated attempts to lose weight by severely restrictive diets, self-induced vomiting, or use of cathartics or diuretics

   Most of us think being bulimic means avoiding weight gain by vomiting. This is probably because 90 percent of bulimics do use this method to control their weight. Some bulimics will stick their finger down their throat. Others will use the end of their toothbrush to induce vomiting. Some just bend over the toilet and vomit without even inducing the gag reflex. Often bulimics drink lots of water or liquids before or between vomiting bouts to make it easier.

   One woman with bulimia was so concerned that she threw up everything she ate in her binges that she put food coloring in her binge foods. For instance, she might make the ice cream she ate first, red, the sugar cookie dough, blue, and then eat four candy bars. That way, she knew when red vomitus appeared, she was throwing up the end of her binge.

   Laxatives, diuretics, and restrictive diets may be used to control weight, as well. While we usually don't think of the person who binges one day and starves the next, as a way of life, to be bulimic, along with the rest of the symptoms, he/she is.

5. Frequent weight fluctuations greater than ten pounds due to alternating binges and fasts

   Bulimics will often have wardrobes in three different sizes because their weight is so unstable. One day their size twelve Calvin Klein jeans may be tight. A week later they may be wearing their tens comfortably. The following week they may be back to their size twelves.

C. Awareness that the eating pattern is abnormal and fear of not being able to stop eating voluntarily.

Bulimics know their eating behavior is not normal. They are very ashamed of the behavior and feel very guilty about it. It's because they find the behavior so weird and disgusting that they carry it out with so much secrecy.

So why don't they stop? Like Nicole, in our case study, they can't. In effect, the bulimic person becomes addicted to eating large quantities of food. He/she becomes hooked on the binge eating and purging.

Recall in the case study where Nicole made herself a good breakfast, a poached egg, a piece of toast and coffee. That was the beginning of several hours of craziness for her. Many bulimics, like Nicole, fear that eating anything will lead to an eating binge.

D. Depressed mood and self deprecating thoughts following eating binges.

Bulimics do not like themselves for binging. They want to stop, but they can't.

E. The bulimic episodes are not due to anorexia nervosa or any known physical disorder.

Bulimics do not purge because they have the flu, a case of food poisoning or have consumed too much alcohol. They self induce vomiting.

Incidence of Bulimia

Twenty to Thirty Percent College Age Women. While the actual incidence of bulimia hasn't been clearly established, evidence exists that bulimia is alarmingly prevalent, even more so than anorexia. The National Association of Anorexia Nervosa and Associated Disorders (ANAD) estimates 20-30 percent of college women engage in the behavior (Neuman & Halvorson, 1983). Craig Johnson (Squire, 1981) director of an eating disorder treatment program at Michael Reese Hospital in Chicago estimates up to 20 percent of college women fit the bulimia criteria.

Incidence Unclear. Exactly how many people are affected remains unclear for a couple of reasons. First, bulimics are very ashamed of their illness. They don't want anyone to know they have such a repulsive problem. They also want to make sure no one finds out they are bulimic. If anyone knew, they wouldn't be able to practice the behavior so comfortably. As a result, even anonymous questionnaires about the disorder aren't answered truthfully by bulimics. Since they don't look sick and their weight is within normal parameters, even friends and family members don't suspect their loved one has bulimia. It's not difficult to find women who have practiced the behavior for a decade or more in secret. In addition, many bulimics previously felt no one experienced such a bizarre problem, so they didn't seek help. Still, bulimics are afraid to expose themselves by seeking treatment because they are afraid no treatment can help them stop binging and purging.

Primarily Women. Bulimia is seen almost exclusively in women. According to ANAD statistics, men represent 5 to 10 percent of the total reported cases. Therefore, for ease, from now on, I will use the female pronouns she and her when discussing the bulimic.

The media has developed a stereotype for the bulimic. She is a white, middle-class woman oriented toward social recognition, academic achievement, and appearance, especially thinness. Many bulimics don't fit this image. Rather, bulimics are found to be a garden-variety population. They run a whole gamut of intelligence, wealth, attractiveness, and ability to function well in life.

Bulimia usually begins in late adolescence or the early twenties. The most frequent age of onset is said to be eighteen years (Neuman & Halvorson, 1983), a time when most people are under a great deal of pressure to make major life decisions and transitions. However, bulimia can also occur at younger ages.

Cause of Bulimia

Unknown. Probably one of the most repeatedly asked questions is, why do people ever develop something like bulimia? Unfortunately, the answer to this question is not known.

Weight Loss. Weight loss appears to be a major factor in the development of bulimia and is the most apparent precursor to the disorder. Twenty-eight-year-old Adrienne, a public relations agent for a New York museum, began this way[2]:

> I used diet pills to fast for long periods and became elated at the weight loss. I'm five feet two inches and went from 155 to 108 pounds. The vomiting started when I'd get so hungry after fasting that I'd eat until I was ready to burst and, wanting both to relieve my discomfort and

2. Excerpts from *Bulimia the Binge-Purge Compulsion* by Janice M. Cauwels and James E. Mitchell, M.D. Copyright (c) by Janice M. Cauwels. Reprinted by permission of Doubleday & Company, Inc.

control weight, I stuck my finger down my throat. I later learned to vomit just as a reflex action. Being thin was so good for me — I loved it, but with my appetite I wouldn't stay there unless I vomited. I always felt guilty about failing at my diet, and suddenly I was free.

Allow time for friends and family members to discuss weight loss as a cause of bulimia. Ask if any of their bulimics began the behavior following a weight loss.

Diets. Some researchers speculate that a destructive diet may cause malnutrition or depression which in turn triggers the bulimia. However, some bulimic women claim to have dieted sensibly while others have started binging and vomiting after weight loss due to surgery or illness. Rita, a thirty-year-old, high school music teacher became bulimic in this way[3]:

> I've never been more than ten pounds overweight, which is just enough for friends to tease me unmercifully about being plump. I pretended that it didn't bother me, but I was terribly sensitive and felt very self-conscious. The summer of my senior year in high school I had an appendectomy, lost the ten pounds and was blasted off on a giant ego trip because everybody, I mean **everybody,** showered me with praises. The problem was that I couldn't maintain the weight because I hadn't dieted and didn't know how to change my habits to avoid overeating. I felt anxious about that and about other pressures — going away from home for the first time to an Ivy League college and wanting to act very self-confident and strong while I was really insecure about my life and especially my appearance. I felt that I had to look and be perfect to fit in at college, so to stay thin I began vomiting up what I ate. I don't remember where I got the idea; maybe it was from how you're supposed to stick a finger down a child's throat to make it vomit if it swallows poison. That started a habit that would plague me on and off the next twelve years. And doing it — even **thinking** about it — was so ugly to me!

Allow time for friends and family members to discuss how dieting may be a factor in the development of bulimia. Ask if any of their bulimics began the behavior following weight loss due to an illness or operation.

Stressful Life Situations. The presence of stressful life situations along with no coping skills may play a role. Denise, a thirty-eight-year-old gynecologist, became bulimic when she had several pressures pile upon her at once[4]:

---

3. Excerpts from *Bulimia the Binge-Purge Compulsion* by Janice M. Cauwels and James E. Mitchell, M.D. Copyright (c) 1983 by Janice M. Cauwels. Reprinted by permission of Doubleday & Company, Inc.

4. Excerpts from *Bulimia the Binge-Purge Compulsion* by Janice M. Cauwels and James E. Mitchell, M.D. Copyright (c) 1983 by Janice M. Cauwels. Reprinted by permission of Doubleday & Company, Inc.

I had always had a weight problem. I was one of your perfectionistic children, never angry, hostile, or upset, always doing everything right. I was too good a girl to try liquor or drugs and always used food instead. The bulimia goes way back to when I had broken off with my fiancé and started out in private practice. A lot of new things were happening all at once, and I lost a lot of weight, but not with vomiting. I thought this was the magical answer—practice in San Francisco, new apartment, new figure—now I thought I would find the man of my dreams, and all kinds of magical things would happen. As I slowed down from all the energy of being really too thin for the first time, I thought I was the perfect woman. I was emaciated and thought I looked like a model. Things slowed down; the office fell through; the man of my dreams turned out to have lots of money and little emotional depth. I was angry about all this and started to overeat again. Somebody at a party suggested that I could vomit, and it sounded like a good idea. It became a terrible habit that I usually indulged in at around 2 A.M.

Allow time for friends and family members to discuss how stressful life situations may play a role in the development of bulimia. Ask if any of their bulimics were under a lot of stress when they began the behavior.

Fear of Rejection. A fear of rejection is also frequently discussed as a source of bulimic symptoms. Perceived or actual rejection by the opposite sex may precipitate the onset of the disorder. Female bulimics often want desperately to please the men in their lives yet don't believe they have the ability to. They are afraid of not being good enough to please a man. Colleen, a thirty-two-year-old lawyer, attributes her illness to this[5]:

I had thought that my relationship with my boyfriend was going well, but he had been dissatisfied with a lot of things he had never mentioned to me. Finally, one day he asked me to meet him at a restaurant for lunch. Halfway through the meal he started laying all my faults out on the table between the clutter of little dishes. It was one of those elegant restaurants that is very quiet, and I'm sure that some of the other people could hear him. He made it quite clear that he wanted nothing to do with me anymore, asked for the check and left. He had arranged to meet me because he knew that I wouldn't make a scene in public and that he could leave me there when it was over.

I was stunned. I somehow left the restaurant, went home and cried myself sick. I had always had a weight problem and usually handled crises by overeating, but this time I was so upset that I felt as if I were gagging on what I had just eaten. I went to the bathroom, stuck my finger down my throat and brought up the whole lunch. I had not

---

5. Excerpts from *Bulimia the Binge-Purge Compulsion* by Janice and James E. Mitchell, M.D. Copyright (c) 1983 by Janice M. Cauwels. Reprinted by permission of Doubleday & Company, Inc.

digested the food, so it didn't smell terrible, and I wasn't really nauseous. So I got the idea of vomiting to lose weight. I wanted to run away and thought of this in terms of getting out of my body by losing weight and leaving my present body behind. The next day I went and got my hair cut in a completely different style, bought all kinds of makeup and started vomiting up everything I ate. I was determined that I would never again look in the mirror and see the woman my boyfriend had rejected.

Allow time for friends and family members to discuss how rejection may play a role in the development of bulimia. Ask if any of their bulimics began the behavior because of rejection by a boyfriend or other male.

Many Other Factors. Other factors which appear to play an important role in the development of bulimia are low self-esteem, social emphasis on slimness, certain family characteristics, a lack of assertiveness, and a variety of biological considerations.

There are other people who have the same problems that have been suggested as potential causes of bulimia, like diminished sense of self-esteem, an underlying fear of rejection, and a fear of being unable to resolve their problems in an effective way. Yet they don't develop bulimia.

There is still much speculation about what causes bulimia. Nothing is totally clear. It's not likely that it's caused by any one single factor. More likely, a number of factors working together are involved in the development of bulimia.

Summary

Summarize session's discussion. Ask for questions or comments.

Helping the Bulimic Get Better Schedule

Understanding What Bulimia Is

This session is designed to help you:

1. become knowledgeable about what bulimia is, its causes, and incidence.
2. meet other friends and family members who are unable to manage the problems produced by being involved with a bulimic.

More About Bulimia

This session is designed to help you:

1. gain information about the effects of bulimia.
2. become knowledgeable about treatment options for bulimia.
3. assist your bulimics in getting professional help for their eating disorder.

Coping with Food Situations Involving Your Bulimic

This session is designed to help you:

manage food situations involving your bulimics so that their recovery is supported and your own needs are satisfied.

Dealing with the Bulimic's Failure to Be Abstinent

This session is designed to help you:

manage the problems resulting from being involved with a practicing bulimic.

Helping the Bulimic Be Abstinent

This session is designed to help you:

support your bulimic's recovery.

Book List

Barrile, J. (1983). *Confessions of a closet eater.* Wheaton, IL: Tyndale.

Boskind-White, M., & White, W. (1986). *Bulimarexia the binge/purge cycle.* New York: W. W. Norton.

Bruch, H. (1978). *The golden cage: The enigma of anorexia nervosa.* Cambridge, MA: University Press.

Cauwels, J.M. (1983). *Bulimia the binge-purge compulsion.* Garden City, NY: Doubleday.

Chernin, K. (1981). *The Obsession.* Scranton, PA: Harper & Row.

Dowling, C. (1981). *The cinderella complex: Women's hidden fear of independence.* New York: Summit Books.

Freed, A. (1976). *T.A. for teenagers.* Los Angelos, CA: Price/Stern/Sloan.

Garfinkel, P., & Garner, D. (1982). *Anorexia nervosa a multi-dimensional perspective.* New York: Brunner/Mazel.

Hall, L. (1980). *Eat without fear.* Santa Barbara, CA: Gurze Books.

Hall, L., & Cohn, L. (1986). *Bulimia: A guide to recovery: Understanding and overcoming the binge-purge syndrome.* Santa Barbara, CA: Gurze Books.

Heater, S.H. (1983). *Am I still visible.* White Hall, VA: Whitehall.

Kaplan, J. (1980). *A woman's conflict with food.* West Nyaek, NY: Prentice Hall.

Kinoy, B.P., Miller, E.B., Atchley, J.A. & the Book Committee of the American Anorexia/Bulimia Association. (1984). *When will we laugh again?* New York: Columbia University Press.

Levenkron, S. (1982). *Treating and overcoming anorexia nervosa.* New York: Charles Scribner.

Liu, A. (1979). *Solitaire: A young woman's triumph over anorexia nervosa.* New York: Harper and Row.

Milman, M. (1980). *Such a pretty face: Being fat in America.* New York: Berkley Books.

Minu Chin, S. (1978). *Psychosomatic families.* Cambridge, MA: Harvard University Press.

O'Neill, C.B. (1982). *Starving for attention.* Scranton, PA: Continuum Books.

Orbach, S. (1978). *Fat is a feminist issue.* New York: Berkley Books.

Palmer, R.L. (1980). *Anorexia nervosa: A guide for sufferers and their families.* New York: Penguin Books.

Pope, H.G., Jr., & Hudson, J.I. (1985). *New hope for binge eaters: Advances in the understanding and treatment for bulimia.* Scranton, PA: Harper & Row.

Powers, P. (1980). *Obesity — the regulation of weight.* Baltimore, MD: Williams & Wilkins.

Roth, G. (1982). *Feeding the hungry heart.* New York: Bobbs-Merril.

Sandbek, T.J. (1986). *The deadly diet: Recovery from anorexia and bulimia.* Oakland, CA: New Harbinger.

Sours, J.A. (1980). *Starving to death in a sea of objects.* San Mateo, CA: Aronson.

Squire, S. (1983). *The slender balance.* New York: Putnam.

Stunkard, A.J. (1979). *The pain of obesity.* Palo Alto, CA: Bull.

Vincent, L.M. (1979). *Competing with the sylph; Dancers and the pursuit of the ideal body form.* Kansas City, KS: Andrews and McMeel.

Vredevelt, P.W., & Whitman, J.R. (1985). *Walking a thin line: Anorexia and bulimia, the battle can be won.* Portland, OR: Multnomah.

Articles from Popular Magazines

Bayer, A.E. (1984, November/December). Eating out of control: anorexia and bulimia in adolescents. *Children Today,* pp. 6-11.

Bernstein, F.A. (1986, November 17). Bulimia: A Woman's terror [case of D. de Garmo]. *People Weekly,* pp. 36-41.

Binge and purge: Road back from bulimia. (1984, October 8). *U.S. News & World Report,* p. 62.

Boskind-White, M., & White, W.C. Jr. (1983, May). Bingeing & purging [excerpt from Bulimarexia]. *Glamour,* pp. 258-259+.

Brenner, M. (1980, June). Bulimarexia. *Savvy: The Magazine for Executive Women,* pp. 54-59.

Bulimia and young women. (1982, June). *USA Today,* p. 6.

Bulimia: The new danger in dieting. (1982, March) *Harpers Bazaar,* pp. 148+.

Eating binges. (1980, November 17). *Time,* p. 94.

Erens, P. (1985, October). Bodily harm: Help for women trapped in the binge-purge cycle. *Ms.,* pp. 62-63+.

Farley, D. (1986, May). Eating disorders: When thinness becomes an obsession. *FDA Consumer,* pp. 20-23.

Fischer, A. (1982, January). Do you stuff yourself one moment and starve yourself the next? *Seventeen,* pp. 106-107+.

Folkenberg, J. (1984, March). Bulimia: Not for women only. *Psychology Today,* p. 10.

Freifeld, K., & Engelmayer, S. (1983, April). How do bulimia patients spell relief? M-A-O. *Health,* pp. 10+.

Herbert, W. (1983, May 14). Modeling bulimia [animal model: research by James Biggs and others]. *Science News,* p. 316.

Hogan, M.B. (1986, October). The nightmare of disturbed eating. *Teen,* pp. 27-8+.

Horosko, M. (1984, February). Eating disorders, part two: Consuming too much [dancers]. *Dance Magazine,* pp. 88-89.

Kohn, V. (1987, February). The body prison: A bulimic's compulsion to eat more, eat less, add muscle, get thinner [case of Christine Bergel]. *Life,* p. 44.

Mackey, A. (1983, April). Bulimia: the diet danger. *Teen,* pp. 4+.

Mayer, A. (1982, July). The gorge-purge syndrome. *Health,* pp. 50-52.

McCoy, C.R. (1984, August 13). A one time olympic gymnast overcomes the bulimia that threatened her life. *People Weekly,* pp. 68+.

McCoy, K. (1982, July). Are you obsessed with your weight? *Seventeen,* pp. 80-81.

Neil, J. (1980, November 3). Eating their cake and having it too [bulimarexia]. *Maclean's,* pp. 51-2.

Ollendick, T.H. (1985, July 29). Busting the bulimia epidemic. [Study by Kathleen J. Hart and Thomas H. Ollendick]. *Science News,* p. 56.

O'Neil, C.B. (1982, November). Starving for attention. *McCalls,* pp. 118-119+.

Rosen, B. (1982, December). A love/hate affair with my body: the story of a food addict. *Mademoiselle,* pp. 141-143.

Schidkraut, M.L. (1982, April). Bulimia: The secret dieter's disease. *Good Housekeeping,* p. 239.

Simon, N. (1982, December). What the experts say about food abuse. *Mademoiselle,* pp. 143 +.

Snyder, F., & Levy, K.G. (1984, January). Slaying the food monster: Help for bulimics. *USA Today,* pp. 74-76.

Squire, S. (1983, October). Is the binge-purge cycle catching? [excerpt from the Slender Balance]. *Ms.,* pp. 41-43 +.

Teenagers diet in dangerous ways. (1986, September). *Prevention,* p. 10.

The hungries [norepinephrine receptors and appetite disorders; interview with S. Leibowitz]. (1984, April). *Health,* pp. 10 +.

White, W.C., & Boskind-White, M. (1981). An experiential-behavior approach to the treatment of bulimarexia. *Psychotherapy: Theory, Research and Practice,* pp. 4, 501-507.

Why women starve and binge [views of Vivian Meehan]. (1985, April). *McCalls,* p. 72.

Young, N. (1979, September). Full stomachs and empty lives; bulimarexia. *Glamour,* pp. 204 +.

You think a friend has an eating disorder — what should you do? (1985, March). *Glamour,* p. 74.

Homework: Understanding What Bulimia Is

Record in writing or on tape each day for the next seven days, every time you hear or see something about dieting, weight, body size, figure, reducing, physical appearance, being fat or thin. Record each time a friend or family member, stranger, or colleague mentions one of these topics. Record each time it is discussed on radio or TV, in the newspaper, in a magazine, in a book or anywhere else.

MORE ABOUT BULIMIA

Instructional Objectives

This session is designed to help significant others to:

1. gain information about the effects of bulimia.
2. become knowledgeable about treatment options for bulimia.
3. assist their bulimics in getting professional help for their eating disorder.

Learner Outcomes

After completing this session, significant others should be able to:

1. summarize the physical effects of bulimia.
2. discuss the psychological aspects of bulimia.
3. discuss treatments for bulimia.
4. evaluate methods of treatment used for bulimia.
5. list bulimia treatment options available in the community.
6. support their bulimic in getting treatment or continuing to participate in treatment.

Presession Activities

Facilitator
— obtains Ann Fischel's (1982) film, *I Don't Have to Hide*. This film may be rented from the Anorexia Nervosa Aid Society of Massachusetts, Inc., Box 213, Lincoln Center, MA 01773. Their phone number is (313) 259-9767. Also, often community libraries will add this film to their collection of films if it is requested.
— prepares list of local eating disorder programs or providers.
— obtains literature about local eating disorder programs.
— may ask representatives from local eating disorder programs to discuss their services at this session.

Activities

Facilitator
— welcomes program participants
— gives out name tags

Group members
— share their immediate concerns
— discuss home assignment

Facilitator	— introduces lecture on bulimia and its treatment
	— provides information about physical and psychological effects of bulimia
	— introduces the film, *I Don't Have to Hide*
Group members	— watch the film, *I Don't Have to Hide*
	— discuss the film, *I Don't Have to Hide*
Facilitator	— shares information about local treatment programs for bulimia
	— may have representatives from eating disorder programs discuss their services
Group members	— exchange their treatment program experiences with the group
Facilitator	— summarizes session's happenings
	— gives home assignment
	— describes upcoming week's topic

Handout Materials

Bulimia Outline Continued
Bulimia Treatment List (to be prepared by group facilitator)
Comparison of Treatment Programs Chart
Eating Disorder Assistance Groups
Homework
Name Tags

Audiovisual Aids

I Don't Have to Hide — film

Visual Aids

Bulimia Outline Overhead
Pamphlets, Brochures and Materials from Bulimia Treatment Programs
    in the Community

Equipment

Film Projector
Overhead Projector
Chalkboard

References

Refer to references used in Lesson Understanding What Bulimia Is

Bulimia Outline Continued

IV. Physical effects of bulimia
   A. Severity of consequences
      1. Amount and types of food
      2. Frequency of purges
      3. Eating patterns
   B. Effects of vomiting
      1. Anemia
      2. Rupture of heart or esophagus
      3. Electrolyte imbalance
         a. Weakness and paralysis
         b. Irregular heart rhythm
         c. Gastrointestinal disease
         d. Kidney problems
      4. Vomiting blood
      5. Sore throats
      6. Difficulty breathing and swallowing
      7. Irregular periods
      8. Swollen salivary glands
      9. Stomach cramps and ulcers
     10. Overall poor health
     11. Tremors, dizziness, tiredness, and apathy
     12. Broken blood vessels
     13. Headaches
     14. Blotchy skin
     15. Irreversible tooth damage
   C. Laxative and diuretic abuse
      1. Diuretics
         a. Kidney damage
         b. Water retention when stop use
      2. Laxatives
         a. Chemical upsets
         b. Bowel tumors
         c. Heart flutters
         d. Dehydration
         e. Ruin normal bowel function
   D. Other physical problems
      1. Improper nourishment
      2. Death

V. Psychological aspects of bulimia
  A. Worse than physical effects
  B. *I Don't Have to Hide*
VI. Treatment
  A. Features of each treatment program
  B. Comparison between treatment programs

Bulimia Lecture Continued

Physical Effects[6]

Severity of Consequences. Although not all bulimics become ill, the list of complications resulting from bulimia is impressive, and professionals don't know whether the body can restore itself to normal once the bulimic becomes abstinent. How severe the consequences of the binging and purging are will depend on a couple of things:

1. The amount and type of food retained. For example, does the bulimic vomit after every meal or only after carbohydrate binges?
2. The frequency of the purges. Is the bulimic vomiting once a week or every day and, if every day, is it once a day or ten times a day?
3. On eating patterns. For instance, does the bulimic eat nutritious meals in addition to her binging or does she alternate between binging on junk food and fasting.

Effects of Vomiting. Theoretically, the long-term effects of the vomiting can range from anemia to rupture of the heart or esophagus. Researchers report fertility may be affected and about half of all bulimics show electrolyte imbalances. Electrolytes are the chemicals that regulate heart and muscle function. The loss of body fluids and electrolytes through vomiting can cause low potassium levels in the blood. This can produce problems ranging from weakness to paralysis, irregular heart rhythm, gastrointestinal disease, and kidney problems. One woman was reported to develop kidney failure after eight years of self-induced vomiting.

Bulimics report vomiting up blood and having chronic sore throats and difficulty in breathing and swallowing. Their periods become irregular. Their parotid glands, the salivary glands in front of each ear, enlarge.

In addition, bulimics feel more obvious effects of their purging. They report stomach cramps, ulcers, and often digestive problems. Those bulimics who stop binging and purging often find themselves constipated. Some end up sick in bed as their bodies go through withdrawal symptoms after prolonged abuse. There are bulimics who binge and vomit with no ill effects, while others experience overall poor health and constant physical problems. They complain of dizziness, weakness,

---

6. Excerpts from *Bulimia the Binge-Purge Compulsion* by Janice M. Cauwels and James E. Mitchell, M.D. Copyright (c) 1983 by Janice M. Cauwels. Reprinted by permission of Doubleday & Company, Inc.

tremors, tiredness, apathy, and irritability. They develop broken blood vessels under their eyes and their necks and suffer from headaches. Their skin becomes grayish and blotched with acne and other sores that don't heal. Since dieting lowers metabolic rate, their bodies immediately store any food they do retain as fat. Ironically, the bulimic's desire to stay attractively slim by vomiting ruins her appearance in other aspects.

Probably the most common effect of self-induced vomiting is irreversible tooth damage caused by the sweet foods that bulimics eat, the acidic vomitus washing over their teeth and the fruit juices or carbonated beverages that many of them drink to relieve their excessive thirst. It's not hard to find bulimic women who have had abscesses, mouth sores, and various problems requiring full sets of crowns, several root canals, and other dentistry costing thousands of dollars.

Laxative and Diuretic Abuse. Although the consequences of vomiting can be more obvious, abuse of laxatives and diuretics can be just as hazardous. Diuretic abuse can damage the kidneys and result in dependency that causes water retention once the diuretics are stopped. Excessive use of laxatives causes a variety of chemical upsets, along with pain, disorders, and infections; it has also been associated with both benign and malignant bowel tumors. Some laxative abusers complain that their hearts flutter for hours after a laxative purge. Like diuretics and vomiting, laxatives can cause massive dehydration. They can also ruin normal bowel functioning.

Other Physical Problems. Besides all these problems caused by their purgative methods, bulimics obviously don't get proper nourishment, regardless of whether or not they resort to fasting.

You probably wonder, what is the bottom line of all this? Can the bulimic's symptoms, obvious or not, eventually kill? Certainly stuffing oneself has its dangers. The media described a twenty-four year-old woman in London who ate herself to death after three days of fasting. She swallowed nearly twenty pounds of food, damaging the walls of her stomach and intestines so badly that doctors were unable to save her. Another woman reported was admitted to a hospital in the Midwest. Her stomach was so swollen by a binge, it threatened to burst for twenty-four hours. Finally, she was able to make herself vomit.

Vomiting can be just as life threatening. Many bulimics report being haunted by the idea of strangling on their vomitus and dying in the bathroom. Vomiting may also produce a deficiency in potassium. It can cause cardiac arrest. Allow time for group members to discuss how the binging and purging has affected their bulimics physically.

Psychological Effects

Even if they aren't done in by their physical problems, bulimics risk endangering themselves because of their chronic depression. One of the anorexia associations was founded by the father of a bulimic woman who killed herself shortly after her twenty-first birthday.

Worse than Physical Effects. Most bulimics find the psychological aspects of the bulimia to be worse than the physical effects. The film "I Don't Have to Hide" illustrates some of the psychological dimensions of the disorder. Note them as we watch it.

"I Don't Have to Hide." Show the film "I Don't Have to Hide." Discuss the effects of Cope's nine-year bout with bulimia. Ask, why do you think Cope started binging and purging? What negative outcomes did Cope experience from the bulimia? What made Cope stop the behavior? What problems did Cope experience once she decided to stop the behavior? What similarities existed between Cope and the other women in her therapy group?

Treatment

Program Features. If the "Helping the Bulimic Get Better" program is being offered in conjunction with a treatment program for bulimics, discuss this treatment program. Discuss the components of the treatment program, its effectiveness and how it compares to other programs.

If the "Helping the Bulimic Get Better" program is being offered independent of any treatment for bulimics, treatment may be addressed a couple of ways.

One route is to request that representatives from eating disorder treatment programs in the area discuss their treatment methods at a session of the "Helping the Bulimic Get Better" program. They may be asked to make individual presentations about their programs or be a member of a panel discussion.

Another option is for the group facilitator to collect information about treatment programs offered in the area and present the findings to the group. A third option is to assign group members this task. It may be given as a home assignment for week one.

Comparison Between Programs. The following questions may be used to gather information about treatment programs being offered in the area.

1. What does the program's treatment consist of?
2. Are topics such as nutrition/meal planning; bulimia's definition, cause, incidence, effects, treatment; body imagery; developing self-esteem; managing stress; exercise; relapse planning and creating a support system addressed?
3. How are dining experiences handled?
4. Is each client's medical and dental status assessed?
5. Does treatment involve drug, individual, or group therapy?
6. How long does the program last?
7. How often are program meetings?
8. Is treatment in or out patient?
9. Is abstinence required by clients?
10. Is the bulimic's family included in therapy?
11. Is there any follow up care after the bulimic completes the program?
12. How long has the program been operating?
13. How effective has the program been in treating its clients?
14. How does this programs' recovery rate compare with other programs?
15. Who is the staff?
16. What are the staff's qualifications?
17. How much time does the bulimic spend with each staff member?
18. What is the cost of the program?
19. Does insurance cover program expenses?
20. Is financial assistance available for the program?
21. How often are clients admitted to the program?
22. Why is this program better than any other program?
23. What are the weaknesses of the program?

Once information has been collected about area programs, compare the features of each. A chart has been provided to assist in this task.

Comparison of Treatment Programs Chart

Program Number	1	2	3	4	5
Program Features					
Nutrition/meal planning					
Bulimia information					
Body image					
Self esteem					
Stress					
Exercise					
Relapse plan					
Support system					
Dining experiences					
Medical					
Dental					
Drug therapy					
Individual therapy					
Group therapy					
Length					
Meeting schedule					
In/out patient					
Abstinence requirement					
Family					
After care					
Existence					
Effectiveness					
Staff					
Cost/Insurance					
Admittance					
Strengths					
Weaknesses					
Other					

Program No.	Name	Contact Person	Phone Number
1			
2			
3			
4			
5			

Comments

Eating Disorder Assistance Groups

American Anorexia/Bulimia Association, Inc.
133 Cedar Lane
Teaneck, New Jersey 07666
Tel. (201) 836-1800

Anorexia Nervosa and Related Eating Disorders, Inc. (ANRED)
P.O. Box 5102
Eugene, Oregon 97405
Tel. (503) 344-1144

National Anorexic Aid Society, Inc. (N.A.A.S.)
5796 Karl Rd.
Columbus, Ohio 43229
Tel. (614) 436-1112

National Association of Anorexia Nervosa and Associated Disorders
(A.N.A.D.)
Box 7
Highland Park, Illinois 60035
Tel. (312) 831-3438

Bulimia Anorexia Self Help
6125 Clayton Ave.
Suite 215
St. Louis, Missouri 62139
Tel. (314) 991-2274

Overeaters Anonymous
4025 Spencer St.
Suite 203
Torrance, California 90503
Tel. (213) 542-8363

Homework: More About Bulimia

1. Inquire about what your bulimic is doing to get better. If he/she is currently involved in treatment and satisfied with it, volunteer support in his/her continuation. If he/she isn't currently involved in treatment or isn't satisfied with his/her treatment, share the options we have discussed with him/her. Offer your assistance in helping him/her get into treatment.
2. Record on tape or in writing how you handled the situation. Record your bulimic's reaction. Record what further actions you plan to take to support him/her getting into treatment or continuing to participate in it.

COPING WITH FOOD SITUATIONS INVOLVING THE BULIMIC

Instructional Objective

This session is designed to help significant others manage food situations involving their bulimic so that their bulimic's recovery is supported and their own needs are satisfied.

Learner Outcomes

After completing this session, significant others should be able to:

1. list problems involving the purchase, preparation, service, storage and consumption of food that may result by being involved with a bulimic.
2. describe alternative methods for handling problematic food situations so that the bulimic's recovery is supported and their own needs are satisfied.

Presession Activities

Facilitator	— becomes familiar with conducting role-playing. Shaftel and Shaftel's (1976, 1982) books on role-playing serve as good references.

Activities

Facilitator	— welcomes program participants
	— gives out name tags
Group members	— share their immediate concerns
	— discuss home assignment
Facilitator	— introduces the evening's problem
	— describes the procedures for role-playing
	— discusses how effective role-playing is in solving problems like the ones this group is facing
	— guides role-playing
Group members	— participate in role-playing
Facilitator	— summarizes session's happenings
	— gives home assignment
	— describes upcoming week's topic

Handout Materials

Homework
Name Tags

Equipment

Chalkboard

Room Arrangement

Chairs in a semicircle
Additional chairs to be used in role-playing

References

American Psychiatric Association. (1980). *Diagnostic and statistical manual of mental disorders* (3rd edition). Washington, D.C.: Author.

Boskind-White, M., & White, W. C., Jr. (1983). *Bulimarexia the binge/purge cycle.* New York: W.W. Norton.

Cauwels, J.M. (1983). *Bulimia the binge-purge compulsion.* New York: Doubleday.

Fischel, A. (Producer & Director). (1982). *I don't have to hide.* [Film]. Jamaica Plains, NY: Fanlight Productions.

Goff, G.M. (1984). *Bulimia: The binge-eating and purging syndrome.* Center City, MN: Hazelden.

Hawkins, R.C., Freemouw, W.J. & Clement, P.F. (1984). *The binge-purge syndrome.* New York: Springer.

Kinoy, B.P., Miller, E.B., Atchley, J.A., & Book Committee of the American Anorexia/Bulimia Association. (1984). *When will we laugh again?* New York: Columbia University Press.

Neuman, P.A. & Halvorson, P.A. (1983). *Anorexia nervosa and bulimia.* New York: Van Nostrand Reinhold.

Shaftel, F.R. & Shaftel, G. (1982). *Role-playing for social values: decision making in the social studies.* Englewood Cliffs, NJ: Prentice Hall.

Shaftel, F.R. & Shaftel, G. (1976). *Role-playing in the curriculum* (2nd edition). Englewood Cliffs, NJ: Prentice Hall.

Squire, S. (1981, October). Why thousands of women don't know how to eat normally anymore. *Glamour,* pp. 245, 309-311.

Role-Playing Coping with Food Situations

Introducing the Problem

As you know, beginning this week and in the next two weeks, we'll take a look at some of the problems friends and family members face by being involved with a bulimic. This week we'll look at problems regarding coping with food situations. We'll attempt to identify alternative ways to handle problematic food situations.

Then we'll examine the consequences that result from our behaviors. We'll do this through role-playing. By role-playing these situations, we'll be able to become more aware of various ways to handle problematic food situations. Unlike real life, we'll get a second chance, actually as many chances as we want to handle the situations.

This evening we'll attempt to deal with problems revolving around food situations the Johnsons didn't know how to manage. The Johnson family consists of Mom and Dad Johnson, Kathy, the youngest in the family, she's fifteen; Tom, the middle child, he's seventeen; and Mary, the oldest, she's twenty-two. The Johnsons found themselves faced with several predicaments regarding food and their bulimic they didn't know how to handle. They occurred all in the same day. It was Thanksgiving.

Let's begin with a description of what Thanksgiving is like at their home. As you listen to the description of this family's "turkey day," try to visualize it. Then we will actually participate in Thanksgiving at their home.

Description of Thanksgiving at the Johnsons'

Over the years, Thanksgiving rituals at the Johnsons's house have been refined to a "T." Their immediate family begins the day bright and early with breakfast. By tradition, it consists of hot, freshly baked caramel rolls and raisin rolls, glazed with frosting, coffee, orange juice, and milk. By ten o'clock, a parade of friends and relatives begin to arrive. They come and go throughout the day.

As custom demands, at the sight of the first guests, two large silver platters filled with an assortment of bars and cookies are placed in the living room. One platter of goodies is placed on the table in front of the couch and the other platter is placed on the big round oak table in the center of the room. They will stay right in these spots all day until dinner is served at four o'clock. They will only be moved to be passed or replenished. That's the custom. On each little side table, there is a dish of peanut brittle, mints, fudge, divinity, or nuts.

Along with the goodies, beer, wine, and almost any alcoholic beverage imaginable are served. A nonalcoholic beverage may be obtained, but only by repeatedly insisting that is what one really wants.

Promptly at noon, a lot more plates and bowls filled with all the family's favorites are brought out. They all know precisely what they are going to be. They are the same treats that were served last year, the year before that, and as far back as they can remember. On one platter is a cheese log with all kinds of different crackers. On another platter is smoked fish and deviled eggs. There is a big bowl of ripple potato chips and two smaller bowls of dip. One is creamy garlic and the other is guacamole. There is also a crockpot with meat balls in sweet and sour sauce. A plate of raw vegetables is always included, too. But over the years, it has become only a token plate of carrot and celery sticks. It just did not make sense to any of them to eat vegetables on the only day of the year when there was no need to feel guilty about splurging on high calorie favorites.

By four o'clock lots of friends and relatives have visited. At this time just their immediate family sits down to Thanksgiving dinner. They all know the menu by heart. There's turkey, wild rice dressing, scalloped potatoes, broccoli with cheese sauce, cranberry sauce, tossed salad with homemade thousand island dressing, cloverleaf buns with raspberry jam, assorted pickles, and of course, pumpkin pie with whipped cream for dessert. They all know too, that no matter how full they are from all the goodies and snacks they've eaten, if they don't fill their plates up at least twice it'll be done for them.

Thanksgiving Day

Let's actually go to Thanksgiving at the Johnson home. The whole family is there; Mom, Dad, fifteen-year-old Kathy, seventeen-year old Tom, and twenty-two-year-old Mary. Everything is going to be the same as other years, that is except Mary. A month ago she told them she had started in therapy for her bulimia. Even though she'd had it for five years, it was a surprise to all of them.

Discussion

So far we have a picture of what Thanksgiving Day is like for the Johnson family. It's a big day. Many things could happen in its course. Let's look at some of the things that might happen. We'll examine them in the form of brief stories that stop before they are finished. As I read each story, think how it might end. Then some of you will have a chance to demonstrate what might happen.

Story One

Imagine it's eleven o'clock on Thanksgiving Day at the Johnsons. There's all kinds of company in the living room. Mary walks in. She sits down in the only empty chair. It's right beside the fudge and the peanut brittle. Mary has told all of her immediate family members it's especially hard for her to be around candy. They all know how she used to eat at least ten pieces of fudge on other Thanksgivings. In fact, they used to joke about all the fudge she could eat.

Role-Playing

Begin the discussion with a question. Ask, "What do you think will happen?" or "What would you do if you were Mary's *Mom* in this situation?" Directions are provided for leading the role-playing. Refer to Guidelines for Conducting the Role-Playing at the end of this chapter for assistance in leading the role-playing.

Story Two

Let's repeat the eleven o'clock story, but this time let's give it a little different twist. Once again, there's all kinds of company in the living room when Mary walks in. Again, she sits down in the only empty chair. It's right beside the fudge and the peanut brittle. But this time, after sitting next to the candy for a few minutes, Mary gets up and pulls Mom aside. She tells her she's going home.

Role-Playing

Begin the discussion by asking, "What would you do if Mary had just told you she was leaving the Thanksgiving celebration because all the food was just too much temptation?" Refer to Guidelines for Conducting the Role-Playing at the end of this chapter for further directions on leading role-playing.

Story Three

Now it's dinner time on Thanksgiving Day at the Johnsons. The whole family, Mom, Dad, Mary, Tom, and Kathy are seated. Grace has just been said. As the food is just starting to get passed around the table,

Mary gets up. She takes her empty plate and goes into the kitchen. In a few minutes she returns with a peanut butter sandwich, some carrot and celery sticks, and an apple on it.

Role-Playing

Begin the discussion by asking, "What would you do if Mary sat down next to you with her sandwich, relishes, and fruit at the Thanksgiving table?" "Have any of you been in a similar situation with your bulimic?" Refer to Guidelines for Conducting the Role-Playing at the end of this chapter for further directions on leading role-playing.

Story Four

This is another Thanksgiving dinner situation at the Johnsons. As the bowls and plates of food are being placed on the table, Mary notices the lemon she brought along for her salad is gone. Dad used it for a drink garnish. He hadn't realized it was hers. Mary announces she can't eat her salad without her lemon. She'll just run over to the convenience store to get one. She'll be back in fifteen minutes.

Role-Playing

Begin the discussion with a question. Ask, "If you were *Dad*, what would you do when Mary told you she was going to go get a lemon at the convenience store?" "What do you think will happen?" Refer to Guidelines for Conducting the Role-Playing for assistance in leading the role-playing. It follows.

Guidelines for Conducting the Role-Playing
(Shaftel & Shaftel, 1976 & 1982)

Discussion Leading into Role-Playing

Facilitator: What do you think will happen?

or

What would you do if you were ＿＿＿ in this situation?

or

Have you ever been in a similar situation in which you just didn't know what to do? I have and it's hard. Once . . .

Group: Responses

Selecting the Role-Play Participants

Facilitator: (to the last participant) Would you like to come up here, _____, and be _____? Remember she/he is a _____. Why don't you pick people to play _____ too. You'll need a _____ and a _____ and a _____.

Setting the Stage

Facilitator: Where is this going to take place, _____?
What is it like in this place?
What are you doing?

Preparing the Audience

Facilitator: As those of you who are playing the audience watch, consider whether you think _____'s way of ending the story could really happen. Observe how each of the family members are feeling.

Think about what will happen next. (The audience may be divided into groups. Ask each group to watch one role in order to define feelings, or ways of thinking of the person being portrayed, or what the role player did that helped or didn't help.)

First Enactment

Role Playing:

(Cut the enactment when:
1. behavior proposed is clear
2. enough data has been presented for discussion
3. some insight has been gained
4. the action is going nowhere
5. it's boring
6. an impasse has been reached
7. the actors need help)

Discussion:

Facilitator: Well, _____ has given us one enactment What did you think of it?
What does _____ mean?
Why do you suppose _____ acted this way?
Will this solution work? Why?
Are there any other ways this problem might be solved?

All right, let's try it your way, _____. (Now players are picked and the scene is set; may keep all the actors the same but one.)

Second Enactment

Role Playing:

Discussion Two:

Facilitator: What about this solution? Do you think this could really happen, _____?

What's your opinion, _____?

Are you saying that _____?

How do you feel, _____, _____, _____ or _____?

Why do you feel this way?

What really is happening here?

Would you like to play it the way you think it could happen, _____?

How about it _____?

Don't you think you can be _____ this time?

Third Enactment

Role Playing:

Discussion Three:

Facilitator: What will happen now?

How do you feel about that _____?

Think it through _____, we'll come back to you in a minute.

Are you wondering if this can be worked out?

Why do you suppose _____, _____, _____, or _____ acted this way?

Are the ways we've seen so far the only ways this problem could be dealt with?

Would you act differently? Why?

Could other ways of acting earlier in the story have helped? Why?

Generalization and Evaluation (after each brief story)

Facilitator: It seems to me in a situation like this many different types of action are sometimes taken (write on the chalkboard actions of role played).

What were the consequences of those actions (write on the chalkboard consequences of actions in role-play)?

It seems to me you have been saying . . .

Can someone put together what has been said-suggested?

Why do you suppose people behave one way rather than another?

Do you think a situation like this could happen to you with your bulimic?

Have any of you experienced this situation or a similar situation like this with your bulimics? For instance, have they _____?

If you could manage this situation in the story as you wished, what would you choose to do?

Why do you suppose _____ didn't choose your way?

Managing Three Potential Complications

1. Sense the discussion has aroused *guilt feelings* in the group. Guide the discussion to replace guilt feelings with reassurance that none of us is perfect, but we can improve with experience. Say, "We have all done this at one time or another. Sometimes it is because _____ or _____." Encourage the group to talk about why people do this; how it feels to _____; what can be done to find more comfortable and adequate ways of solving problems.

2. A group member portrays a highly *unacceptable solution*. Accept the enactment matter of factly, saying, _____ has shown us what some people do in this situation. _____ is reminding us these things do happen. In this way the implication is removed that this is the way _____ would behave in real life.

3. An individual needs protection from *group pressure*. The facilitator can support each group member's right to do their own thinking by asking questions such as: Why do you suppose _____ sees this differently from most of you? Can you tell us more about your view _____? Do you think _____ must see this the way you do? Can we gain something from one another's ideas, if we explore our different ways of seeing things rather than insisting on agreement?

Homework:
Coping with Food Situations Involving the Bulimic

1. Have you ever been involved in a situation with your bulimic involving food that you didn't know how to handle? Do you know someone who has? If not, create a situation with a bulimic, involving food, which his/her significant other didn't know how to handle.

2. In writing or on tape describe:
   a. the situation.
   b. how you or the significant other dealt with the situation.
   c. what happened.
   d. two alternative ways you or the significant other could have dealt with this situation.
   e. which alternative do you think is the most acceptable?
   f. why?

DEALING WITH THE BULIMIC'S FAILURE TO BE ABSTINENT

Instructional Objective

This session is designed to help significant others manage problems resulting from being involved with a practicing bulimic.

Learner Outcomes

After completing this session, significant others should be able to:

1. identify problems resulting from their bulimic's eating disorder.
2. describe alternative methods for satisfactorily handling problems produced by their bulimic's eating disorder.
3. list negative feelings like anger, guilt, hurt, frustration, and irritation, which they have when their bulimic fails to be abstinent.
4. discuss appropriate methods for managing their negative feelings which may result when their bulimic binges and/or purges.

Activities

Facilitator	— welcomes program participants
	— passes out name tags
Group members	— share their immediate concerns
	— discuss home assignment
Facilitator	— introduces the evening's problems
	— guides role-playing
Group members	— participate in role-playing
Facilitator	— summarizes session's happenings
	— gives home assignment
	— describes upcoming week's topic

Handout Materials

Homework
Name Tags

Equipment

Chalkboard

Room Arrangement

Chairs in a semi-circle
Additional chairs to be used in role-playing

References

Refer to references used in Lesson Coping with Food Situations

Role-Playing Dealing with the Bulimic's Failure
to Be Abstinent

Introducing the Problem

As you know, recovery for most bulimics will involve reverting back
to previous eating patterns. Dr. Eckert, one of the psychiatrists in the
University of Minnesota's bulimia program says, "Once an individual is
bulimic, there is always a tendency toward bulimia. Bulimia is like cancer or tuberculosis in that it can be arrested and seem cured after a specific period of remission, but the danger of relapse always remains."
Most of us try to block out thoughts of our bulimic ever binging and
purging again. But as much as we hope it won't happen, the possibility
of a relapse is very real.

Tom did experience this situation. I am going to share his story with
you this evening. This story, like the ones from last week, stops before
it's finished. As I read it, think about what you would do if you were in
Tom's place. Following the story, some of you will have a chance to role-
play how Tom might cope with his dilemma.

Story One

My name is Tom. I'm Mary's husband. We've been married three
years. Two months ago Mary told me she was bulimic. That day she
stopped binging and vomiting. She's been abstinent ever since. This
past week I had to go out of town for work. I was able to finish up a day
earlier than I expected. So I decided, I'd just surprise Mary and come
home early. When I got home, to my disappointment, Mary wasn't
there. She'd obviously gone out somewhere. I'd brought her flowers. So
I put them in a vase and got them all set for her. Then I decided to go
ahead and unpack. But when I got to our bedroom, I couldn't help but
see our wastebasket was all filled with candy bar and junk food wrappers.

Role-Playing Ending A

It's an hour later now. Tom and Mary are sitting and chatting. What would you do if you were Tom?

Role-Playing Ending B

It's an hour later now. Tom and Mary are sitting and chatting. Tom tells Mary he found the wastebasket all filled with candy bar and junk food wrappers. Mary denies having eaten the food. She explains to Tom she was cleaning out her drawers and found them. She had hidden them there when she was binging and purging. What would you do if you were Tom?

Role-Playing Ending C

It's an hour later now. Tom and Mary are sitting and chatting. Tom tells Mary he found the wastebasket filled with junk food and candy bar wrappers. Mary tells Tom, that's right, she had a binge and it's all his fault. It never would have happened if he wouldn't have left her alone. What would you do if you were Tom?

Discussion Leading into Role-Playing

Refer to Guidelines for Conducting the Role-Playing in Lesson Coping with Food Situations.

Dealing with the Bulimic's Failure to Be Abstinent
Optional or Additional Role-Plays

Introducing the Problem

Last week we spent Thanksgiving with the Johnsons. Let's return once again to their home on Thanksgiving Day. Recall from last week that the whole family is home for the day; Mom, Dad, fifteen-year-old Kathy, seventeen-year-old Tom, and twenty-two-year-old Mary. This year everything is the same as it's always been. That is with one exception, Mary. A month ago she told her family she had started in therapy for her bulimia. Even though she'd been bulimic for five years, it was a surprise to all of them.

This week, like last week, we'll examine some of the problems the Johnson family face on Thanksgiving Day. The problems will be presented in brief stories that stop before they are finished. As I read each story, think how it might end. Then some of you will have a chance to demonstrate what might happen.

Story One

Let's begin with breakfast. The whole Johnson family is sitting around the kitchen table. Everyone except Mary is eating a piping hot caramel or frosted raisin roll. She is drinking a small glass of orange juice. She told her family she stopped eating sweets when she began therapy because they seemed to set off her binges. Mom Johnson gets up to serve Tom his third roll. She asks if anyone else wants another roll. Mary says, "Ya, I'll have a caramel one."

Role-Playing

Imagine you are Mom. What would you do if Mary asked you for a caramel roll?

Story Two

Now it's dinner time on Thanksgiving Day. Everyone is eating, talking, and having a good time, Mary included. In fact, she's already eaten two heaping plates of food. She's just filled her plate for the third time when she excuses herself to go to the bathroom.

Role-Playing

What would you do if you were Mary's brother, Tom, in this situation? What do you think will happen?

Story Three

Thanksgiving dinner at the Johnsons has just finished. Everyone is helping to clean up. Mary has been elected to clean up the leftover snacks in the living room. Kathy decides to help Mary. But to her surprise, Mary is so busy putting fudge and peanut brittle in a napkin inside her purse, she doesn't even see her.

Role-Playing

Imagine you are Kathy. What would you do if you found Mary putting candy in her purse?

Discussion Leading into Role-Playing

Refer to Guidelines for Conducting the Role-Playing in Lesson Coping with Food Situations.

Homework: Dealing with the Bulimic's Failure to Be Abstinent

Write or tape a story about a significant other who discovers his/her bulimic has returned to binging and vomiting or using laxatives after being abstinent for a few weeks. This may be a real or imagined story.

a. In your story, describe the situation.
b. In your story, describe how the significant other handled the situation.
c. In your story, describe what happened as a result of the significant other's action.
d. Describe two alternative ways the significant other could deal with the slip.
e. Which alternative do you think is most acceptable?
f. Why?

HELPING THE BULIMIC BE ABSTINENT

Instructional Objective

This session is designed to help significant others support their bulimic's recovery.

Learner Outcomes

After completing this session, significant others should be able to:

1. identify behavior they are currently practicing that may be sabotaging their bulimic's recovery.
2. describe supportive behavior which they can substitute for behavior that may be sabotaging their bulimic's recovery.
3. state ways they can support their bulimic's recovery.

Activities

Facilitator	— welcomes program participants
	— passes our name tags
Group members	— share their immediate concerns
	— discuss home assignment
Facilitator	— introduces the evening's problem
	— guides role-playing
Group members	— participate in role-playing
Facilitator	— summarizes session's happenings
	— gives home assignment
	— describes upcoming week's topic
	— makes concluding remarks.
	— schedules follow-up meeting if this is the last session of the program

Handout Materials

Homework
Name Tags
Evaluation Forms—to be completed at home and turned in at the follow-up meeting

Equipment

Chalkboard

Room Arrangement

Chairs in a semicircle
Additional chairs to be used in role-playing

References

Refer to references used in Lesson Plan Coping with Food Situations

Role Playing Helping the Bulimic Be Abstinent

Introducing the Problem

These past two weeks we have spent Thanksgiving day with the Johnsons. In one day, they encountered many situations involving food and their bulimic loved one, Mary, they didn't know how to handle.

This week we are going to spend an evening two weeks before Thanksgiving Day with this family. They are having a family discussion about what to do on Thanksgiving. We'll look at a couple of problems in the form of brief stories that stop before they are finished. Like last week, and the week before, as I read each story, I'd like you to think how it might end. Then some of you will have a chance to demonstrate what might happen.

Two Weeks Before Thanksgiving

So, let's go to the Johnson family discussion. It's taking place two weeks before Thanksgiving. They are all there, Mom and Dad Johnson; Kathy, the youngest daughter; Tom, the middle son; and twenty-two-year-old Mary, who no longer lives at home.

The whole family is together to decide what they should do about Thanksgiving. Mary just told them two weeks ago that she's bulimic and in therapy for it.

Mary begins the discussion. She says she wouldn't miss Thanksgiving with the family for anything. She tells them how much it's always meant to her. She is really looking forward to seeing all the relatives and old family friends. It's just so neat to all be together. She'd really feel bad if she couldn't come.

Story One

This year she won't be able to come though if there are going to be sweets served. That means stuff like the breakfast rolls, the fudge, the peanut brittle, and the pumpkin pie. It would just be too hard for her. Right now, the most important thing in her life is staying abstinent. She hopes they understand.

Role-Playing

Imagine you are a member of the Johnson family. What do you think will happen?

Story Two

Let's go back to the discussion again. Mary has just told her family how she's really looking forward to Thanksgiving and would feel really bad if she couldn't come. She goes on to explain to them though, that it'll really be hard for her to sit at the dinner table with all the bowls and platters of food tempting her. This year, could dinner just be served from the kitchen on plates rather than family style, like it's always been done in the past?

Role-Playing

Have you ever been in a situation like this? What happened?

Story Three

Let's return to the family discussion one more time. Mary begins the discussion once again. She tells her family how important she knows Thanksgiving is to them and how it always has meant a lot to her, too. She goes on to say she realizes all the relatives and family friends are planning on coming, too. She is well aware that this is the only time of the year they get to see a lot of these people. But this year, could the family just skip Thanksgiving and do something else on that day, like drive up north? With her bulimia she really doesn't think she could handle the traditional Thanksgiving without binging.

Role-Playing

What would you do if you were Mary's *Dad* in this situation?

Discussion Leading into Role-Playing

Refer to Guidelines for Conducting the Role-Playing in Lesson Coping with Food Situations.

Helping the Bulimic Be Abstinent — Two

Introducing the Problem

Each of us is involved and some of us live with a bulimic. Many of our bulimics have asked us to change our ways to make recovery easier for them. At times, we may have felt their requests were not reasonable or justified. We may even have felt complying might hinder their recovery. You can probably think of at least one situation like this that you didn't know how to handle. This evening, I'd like to read you a story of a husband who did experience this problem. Like the stories we've read the past two weeks, this one stops before it's finished. As I read the story, think how it might end. Following the story, some of you will have a chance to demonstrate how this husband might manage his problem.

Story

I'm Gary. My wife, Maria, and I have been married five years. The first week we were married, we decided to set aside Sunday night to just stay home. We'd put on our pajamas and spend the evening in front of the TV. I'd make us a big bowl of popcorn. Popcorn is my specialty. No one makes it the way I do. For instance, I sauté fresh minced garlic for the butter even. We've rarely missed a Sunday night of TV and popcorn in the five years we've been married. That is until one month ago. One month ago, Maria told me she was bulimic. She stopped binging and using laxatives that day. It was a Sunday. She asked me if we could stop our Sunday night popcorn from that Sunday on. She said just the smell of it was enough to make her binge. I agreed at the time.

Now I feel differently. I really miss having popcorn on Sunday night, made my special way. I would like to start having it again. I feel Maria is going to be confronted with tempting food situations her whole life. So far she has avoided them. She's not going to be able to do that forever. She just has to learn to control herself in these situations. What would you do if you were Gary in this situation?

Discussion Leading into Role-Playing

Refer to Guidelines for Conducting the Role-Playing in Lesson Coping with Food Situations.

Helping the Bulimic be Abstinent — Three

Introducing the Problem

Bob finds himself faced with a problem involving his bulimic wife, Nancy, similar to that of Gary. Just as in the previous situation, I'll read Bob's story. Like Gary's story, it will stop before it's finished. Think how it might end. Then some of you will have a chance to demonstrate how it might end.

Story

My name is Bob. Nancy and I have been married for eight years. Two months ago, Nancy told me she was bulimic. That day she stopped binging and vomiting. She's been abstinent ever since. I'm the only one she's told about her problem. Last week, the Smiths called. They invited us to go with them to a Chinese New Year's buffet on Saturday night. We told them we'd be delighted. We always thought it would be so much fun. We'd just never gotten around to going, though. They said we'd had them to our house so many times, it would be their treat. It was all set. They'd go ahead and buy the tickets. It's now Saturday morning. Nancy just told me she didn't think she could handle going to a buffet. She asked if I'd mind if we cancelled out on the Smiths for the Chinese buffet tonight. What would you do if you were Bob in this situation?

Note: In this situation, Nancy is not only asking her husband to deprive himself of an enjoyable evening with friends he's been looking forward to, but also to inconvenience other people who are not aware of her problem.

Discussion Leading into Role-Playing

Refer to Guidelines for Conducting the Role-Playing in Lesson Coping with Food Situations.

Homework: Helping the Bulimic Be Abstinent

Has your bulimic asked you to do something to support his/her recovery you thought was unreasonable? Do you know someone who has been in this situation? If not, create a situation where a significant other thinks his/her bulimic is asking him/her to do something to support his/her recovery that is unreasonable. Write or tape the assignment.

   a. Describe the situation.
   b. How did the significant other deal with the situation?
   c. What happened?
   d. Describe two alternative ways the significant other could deal with the situation.
   e. Which do you think is most acceptable?
   f. Why?

Chapter III

IMPLEMENTING A BULIMIA ASSISTANCE PROGRAM—PART TWO

THIS CHAPTER contains five optional lesson plans. They are titled: Removing Blame, Developing Trust, Managing Negative Feelings, Dealing with Problems, and Becoming a Healthy Eater. They are designed to help significant others:

1. stop blaming themselves or others for their bulimic's eating disorder.
2. gain trust in their bulimic.
3. manage negative feelings produced by being involved with a bulimic.
4. deal with bulimia-related problems.
5. develop healthy eating patterns.

The first, four lesson plans solve problems through role-playing. The fifth lesson plan consists of information sharing by the facilitator. Techniques used in this lesson plan are lecturing and discussion.

The optional lesson plans may be substituted for lesson plans in the five-week "Helping the Bulimic Get Better" program. They may be used to extend the five-week program to a six, seven, eight, nine or ten-week program or they may be offered as Part Two of the "Helping the Bulimic Get Better" program. Another possibility is to pool these lesson plans with ones from the "Helping the Bulimic Get Better" program. Then offer a series of day-long or weekend workshops for friends and families of bulimics.

When selecting the program format for implementing the lesson plans, recognize active participation in role-playing will be enhanced if significant others feel comfortable with each other. This may be accomplished by asking program participants to introduce and tell a little bit about themselves during the first session of the program. Significant others can also be helped to get to know and feel more at ease with one another by working on tasks with two or three other group members. For this reason, an information sharing session in which the facilitator makes the presentation generally works well for the first session. Solving problems through role-playing is more appropriate for later sessions in the program.

REMOVING BLAME

Instructional Objective

This session is designed to help significant others to stop blaming themselves or others for their bulimic's eating disorder.

Learner Outcomes

After completing this session, significant others should be able to:

1. describe the harm blaming themselves or others for their bulimic's eating disorder produces.
2. list alternatives to blaming themselves or others for their bulimic's eating disorder.
3. evaluate methods to stop blaming themselves or others for their bulimic's eating disorder.

Activities

Facilitator	— welcomes program participants
	— gives out name tags
Group members	— share their immediate concerns
	— discuss the home assignment
Facilitator	— introduces the evening's problem
	— guides role-playing
Group members	— participate in role-playing
Facilitator	— summarizes the session's happenings
	— gives home assignment
	— describes upcoming week's topic

Handout Materials

Homework
Name Tags

Equipment

Chalkboard

Room Arrangement

Chairs in a semicircle
Additional chairs to be used in role-playing

References

Refer to references used in Lesson Coping with Food Situations

Role-Playing Removing Blame

Introducing the Problem

Many significant others blame a specific individual for their bulimic's eating disorder. Some significant others blame themselves and feel everyone else does, too. Overwhelmingly, mothers are given or take responsibility when eating disorders are examined. Not as frequently, but fathers, too, are given or take responsibility for their daughter's/son's eating disorder. Husbands, brothers, sisters, and roommates of the bulimic even are given or take responsibility for the eating disorder.

This evening I'd like to read you a story about a mother who blamed herself and was blamed by others for her daughter's bulimia. Tina, the twin sister of a bulimic named Tammy tells her story. Like the ones we've read in previous weeks, it stops before it's finished. As I read it, think of how it might end. After we've read the story, some of you will have a chance to demonstrate how this story might be ended.

Story

I'm Tina. Tammy is my bulimic twin sister. It's hard to believe she's no longer binging and vomiting. I can't remember when she wasn't.

Even as children we were little fatties. My mom put us on our first diet when we were four. We hadn't even started kindergarten yet. I still remember the big to do she made at meals about Tammy and I drinking skim milk. At the time, it seemed so unfair. Everybody else got to have whole milk. Needless to say, we stayed pudgy.

By third grade, dieting was an accepted way of life for Tammy and me. That was the year we were finally old enough to go for a week's visit to our Dad's parents. We could hardly wait. Just Tammy and I were going. My mom didn't like my Dad's parents, though, so she wasn't too excited about us going. Then, a day before we were to go, Mom and Dad had this big fight. Mom told Dad that Tammy and I had been doing so well on our diets. She knew if he sent us to his mother's, she'd feed us french fries, ice cream, and all the bad stuff we shouldn't have. Just look at what she'd done to his two sisters. They were such beautiful girls, but fat slobs. No wonder they couldn't get husbands. Did he want his daughters to be fatties like them? My mom did let us go to grandma's and grandpa's that summer, but she wasn't happy about it.

Somehow we made it to adolescence. We still had an extra five or ten pounds. That was when Tammy began the binging and vomiting.

We were in the seventh grade. When we came home from school, Tammy would eat a bag of potato chips and a quart of ice cream with chocolate sauce. Then she'd go throw it up.

A few jokes were made about the way Tammy ate, but not too much was thought of it. We'd all seen my Mom eat like this. There were many nights when she'd serve the family a meat and potato dinner and make boiled fish and lettuce for herself. Then about eight o'clock she'd sneak into the kitchen and eat the half pan of bars left from dinner. She loved those one pound Hershey candy bars, too. Lots of times she'd eat a whole one while she watched the 10 p.m. news.

It's been eighteen years since Tammy began binging and vomiting. All of us kids are grown up and living in our own houses now. Tonight, my Mom invited me to have dinner with her and Dad. She said she needed to talk. She said she was feeling like it was all her fault that Tammy became bulimic.

When Tina goes to see her Mom and Dad, her Mom says to her, "Tina, I feel like I was a terrible mother. It's all my fault that Tammy is bulimic." What would you do if you were Tina in this predicament?

Discussion Leading into Role-Playing

Refer to Guidelines for Conducting the Role-Playing in Lesson Coping with Food Situations.

Homework: Removing Blame

Do you blame yourself or someone else for your bulimic's eating disorder? Do you know someone who blames himself/herself or another person for his/her bulimic's eating disorder. If not, create a story about a significant other who blames himself/herself for his/her bulimic's eating disorder or another person. Write or tape the following assignment:

   a. Describe the situation in the story.
   b. Who is blamed for the eating disorder?
   c. Why is this person blamed for the eating disorder?
   d. Describe two ways the significant other could manage these feelings.
   e. Which alternative do you think is most acceptable?
   f. Why?

DEVELOPING TRUST

Instructional Objective

This session is designed to help significant others develop trust in their bulimics.

Learner Outcomes

After completing this session, significant others should be able to:

1. discuss what they can do to gain trust in their bulimic.
2. describe acceptable methods for handling situations in which they question their bulimic's behavior.
3. identify what the effects will be if they continue to question their bulimic's behavior.

Activities

Facilitator	— welcomes program participants
	— passes out name tags
Group members	— share their immediate concerns
	— discuss the home assignment
Facilitator	— introduces the evening's problem
	— guides role-playing
Group members	— participate in role-playing
Facilitator	— summarizes session's happenings
	— gives home assignments
	— discusses upcoming week's topic

Handout Materials

Homework
Name Tags

Equipment

Chalkboard

Room Arrangement

Chairs in a semi-circle
Additional chairs to be used in role-playing

References

Refer to references used in Lesson Coping with Food Situations

Role-Playing Developing Trust

Introducing the Problem

Each of us is involved and some of us live with a recovering bulimic. Since your bulimic loved one stopped binging and using laxatives or vomiting, have you been in a situation where you weren't really sure you believed what he/she said? Yet, you didn't know what you should do about it. Have you ever felt like you didn't know if you'd ever be able to totally trust him/her again? You wanted to trust him/her but you didn't know how to make it happen.

I would like to read you a story this evening about a husband, named John, who faced this problem. The story stops before it's finished. While I am reading the story, try to think of how it might end. Then some of you will have a chance to demonstrate how John might solve his problem.

Story

John and Jill have been married a little over two years. Prior to getting married, they dated for three years. John still remembers the first time they went out to eat together. They went to a typical supper club. Jill ordered the sixteen ounce prime rib dinner. It came with soup, salad bar, bread, and choice of potato. At the salad bar, she heaped her bowl full of all the high calorie salads, like potato salad, macaroni salad, and whipped cream fruit salad. She sawed off a big piece of bread for both John and herself and globbed on lots of butter. She made a second trip back for the beer cheese soup. She ate every bit of what she'd taken. Then to John's amazement she finished her prime rib and the au gratin potatoes that came with her meal. They continued to date and Jill continued to eat. It didn't change after they were married. John was astounded by the amount of food she could eat. She didn't have a weight problem either, maybe an extra pound or two, but that was it. She said she had a fast metabolism.

At times John wondered if Jill was bulimic. He knew all about bulimia. Jill talked a lot about a friend's friend who had it. But he figured, his wife, how could she be bulimic? Besides, he'd never seen her throw up.

A month ago, Jill told him the truth. She was bulimic and had been for eighteen years. That day she was stopping the binging and vomiting.

John's not sure any more though. He never questioned her before. Why would he have? He had no reason to doubt her. But that's no longer the case. Now he knows she lied to him. The loaves of bread she told him she fed the birds, she ate them. The pans of bars and dozens of cookies she told him she took to meetings and parties, she ate them. The leftovers she told him she threw out because they were spoiling, she ate them. The money she told him she lost, got stolen or donated for charity, she bought food with it. The evenings when she told him she worked, she devoted them to eating. All the food she could eat because she had a fast metabolism, what she really had was bulimia. John just wishes he knew what to do. He wonders if there's any best way to handle the dilemma he's facing.

Tonight, he called the Health Club to ask Jill to pick up some milk on the way home. The club attendant informed him Jill wasn't there and hadn't been at all that day. Yet, that's where she had told him she'd be spending the evening. What do you think John should do when Jill comes home?

Discussion Leading into Role-Playing

Refer to Guidelines for Conducting the Role-Playing in Lesson Coping with Food Situations.

Homework: Developing Trust

Since your bulimic loved one told you he/she had stopped binging and purging, have you been in a situation where you really weren't sure you believed what he/she said? Do you know someone who has? If not, create a situation where a friend or family member isn't sure they believe what their bulimic says. Write or tape the following assignment.

a. Describe the situation.
b. How did the significant other deal with the situation?
c. What happened?
d. Describe two alternative ways the significant other could have dealt with the situation.
e. Which alternative do you think is the most acceptable?
f. Why?

MANAGING NEGATIVE FEELINGS

Instructional Objective

This session is designed to help significant others manage feelings of anger, hurt, frustration, humiliation, irritation, indifference, disappointment, and disgust produced by being involved with a bulimic.

Learner Outcomes

After completing this session, significant others should be able to:

1. describe why they have negative feelings toward their bulimic.
2. discuss the consequences feeling negative toward their bulimic produces.
3. examine alternatives to feeling negative toward their bulimic.

Activities

Facilitator	— welcomes program participants
	— passes out name tags
Group members	— share their immediate concerns
	— discuss the home assignment
Facilitator	— introduces the evening's problem
	— guides role-playing
Group members	— participate in role-playing
Facilitator	— summarizes session's happenings
	— gives home assignment
	— describes upcoming week's topic

Handout Materials

Homework
Name Tags

Equipment

Chalkboard

Room Arrangement

Chairs in a semi-circle
Additional chairs to be used in role-playing

References

Refer to references used in Lesson Coping with Food Situations

Role Playing Managing Negative Feelings

Introducing the Problem

Anger, frustration, pain, humiliation, and irritation are some of the feelings significant others experience by being involved with a bulimic. Do any of you have these feelings? How are you managing them?

I'd like to read you a story this evening about a father who experienced some of these feelings. In addition, the father in our story is faced with another problem many significant others involved with bulimics face. He wants to help his bulimic daughter get better, but doesn't know how.

Story

When my daughter, Joan, finished high school she wanted to go to a private women's college out east. It was a dream she'd had since her mother, Doris, and I first started talking about college to her. I just couldn't tell her there was no way I could afford a college like that. I knew it would break her heart. So I decided to do what I swore, no matter what, I'd never do. I went to my wife's older brother and asked him for a loan. He's a wealthy contractor. He never thought I was good enough for Doris. When we were dating, he always told Doris I'd never amount to anything. If she married me, she'd be making a big mistake.

It was a hard exchange to make, but I did it. I gave up my pride for a loan. I knew that was the only way I'd be able to send Joan to her private women's college out east.

I hoped the day would never come that I'd have to go ask Doris's brother for more money. But I knew, it might. Sending Joanie to her private women's college turned out to be much more expensive than we thought. It seemed a week didn't go by that Joan didn't need money for something. She either had to buy books, uniforms or paper supplies, or pay lab fees, linen fees, or typing charges. That's not to mention the cost of her designer clothes, make-up, and hair styles. They came from the most fashionable shops. She said she wished she didn't have to ask us for those things, but if she wanted to be a fashion design major, it was required.

I never did have to go back to Doris's brother for more money. Joan flunked out of college. She said it was her bulimia. I never knew it, but she'd been binging and vomiting since she was thirteen. She said once she got to college it became so bad she could do nothing but eat or think about eating. That's really where all the money went, not to books, lab fees, or clothes. It went to food.

Well, now Joanie is home. It's been a month since she arrived. It's been hard. I really don't know what to do. I don't think I can hack this much longer. Every time I look at Joan, I see Doris's brother. He's smirking at me with that "I knew this would happen" look on his face. When I think I begged that man for money, for what, for nothing.

Then to top it off, Joanie is worse than ever. She just sits at home doing nothing. Some days she won't eat anything all day. Then other days I'll find the garbage can over flowing with the remains from one of her binges. That really t's me off. But if I barely say anything to her, she starts crying. Then I feel even worse. This is really getting unbearable. I just don't know what to do. What would you do if you were Joanie's father in this situation?

Discussion Leading into Role-Playing

Refer to Guidelines for Conducting Role-Playing in Lesson Coping with Food Situations.

Homework: Managing Negative Feelings

Do you feel angry, frustrated, hurt, disappointed, indifferent, humiliated, disgusted, or irritated by things your bulimic has done while he/she was binging and vomiting or using laxatives? Do you know someone who does feel this way because of his/her bulimic's behavior? If not, create a situation involving a significant other in which one or more of these feelings are produced. Write or tape the assignment.

    a. Describe the situation.
    b. How does the significant other feel?
    c. What caused the significant other to feel this way?
    d. Describe two alternative ways to deal with these feelings.
    e. Which alternative do you think is the most acceptable?
    f. Why?

DEALING WITH PROBLEMS

Instructional Objectives

This session is designed to help significant others deal with problems they are experiencing by being involved with a practicing or recovering bulimic.

Learner Outcomes

After completing this session, significant others should be able to:

1. describe one problem they are experiencing by being involved with a practicing or recovering bulimic.
2. list alternative ways to manage the problem.
3. examine possible consequences which may occur as a result of the way they manage the problem.
4. determine the most acceptable methods for managing the problem.

Activities

Facilitator	— welcomes program participants
	— passes out name tags
Group members	— share their immediate concerns
	— discuss home assignments
Facilitator	— introduces the evening's problem
	— asks members to form small groups of three or four
Small groups	— identify one problem they are experiencing by being involved with a bulimic
	— write a story about a friend of family member experiencing a problem with their bulimic that stops before it finishes
Facilitator	— assists small groups with writing their stories
	— reads the small groups' stories to the entire group
Group members	— participate in role-playing
Facilitator	— summarizes session's happenings
	— gives home assignments
	— describes upcoming week's topic

Handout Materials

Homework
Name tags
One note pad for each small group
One pencil for each small group

Equipment

Chairs in a semi-circle
Additional chairs to be used in role-playing

References

Refer to references used in Lesson Coping with Food Situations

Note. This lesson plan may be extended over two weeks or used more than once.

Role-Playing Dealing with Problems

In the past few weeks, we have dealt with problems that friends and family members often experience by being involved with a bulimic. They have included coping with food situations involving the bulimic, dealing with the bulimic's failure to be abstinent, helping the bulimic be abstinent, removing blame, developing trust, and managing negative feelings.

This week we are going to examine other problems you are experiencing by being involved with a practicing or recovering bulimic. Each of you, along with one or two other members of this group, will be able to discuss a problem, other than the ones we've discussed, you are experiencing by being involved with a bulimic. As a small group, you will identify one problem you would like to examine further. Then your group will write a story about a real or imaginary friend or family member who faces this problem. End your story before it finishes or the concerned other takes action to solve the problem. Make the last sentence in each of your stories, what you would do if you were *(name of significant other in the story with the problem)* in (his/her) predicament?

Then I will read each story and some of you will have a chance to demonstrate what might happen.

Discussion Leading into Role-Playing

Refer to Guidelines for Conducting the Role-Playing in Lesson Coping with Food Situations.

Homework: Dealing with Problems

Have you experienced a problem you didn't know how to handle involving your bulimic? Has someone you know experienced a bulimia-related problem he/she didn't know how to deal with? If not, create a situation where a concerned other finds himself/herself in a situation with his/her bulimic he/she doesn't know how to manage. Write or tape the situation.

    a. Describe the situation.
    b. How did the concerned other deal with the situation?
    c. What happened?
    d. Describe two alternative ways the concerned other could deal with the situation.
    e. Which do you think is most acceptable?

BECOMING A HEALTHY EATER

Instructional Objectives

This session is designed to help significant others to:

1. become knowledgeable about what healthy eating is.
2. be able to implement a healthy eating plan for themselves.

Learner Outcomes

After completing this session, significant others should be able to:

1. describe what an adequate diet is for themselves.
2. explain how the Exchange Lists for Meal Planning work.
3. list the foods contained in each exchange list of the Exchange Lists for Meal Planning.
4. identify nutrient excesses or deficiencies which may produce physical complications.
5. name foods high in fat, sodium, fiber, and sugar.
6. state abbreviations used on labels for vitamins and minerals.
7. make a healthy eating plan for themselves.
8. identify obstacles which may hinder following a healthy eating plan.
9. describe how friends and family members can support their healthy eating patterns.

Pre-Session Activities

Facilitator

— asks a Registered Dietitian to conduct the Healthy Eating session.
— provides Dietitian with the height, weight, daily activities and special dietary considerations of each program participant.
— obtains a copy of the *Exchange Lists for Meal Planning* (American Diabetic Association Inc., and the American Dietetic Association (ADA), 1986) for each program participant. Write the ADA at 208 South LaSalle Street, Suite 1100, Chicago, IL 60604-1003 or call ADA at (312) 899-0040 for the pamphlets. The pamphlet's cost is $1.25 for nonmembers and $1.00 for ADA members.

Registered Dietitian — calculates the number of exchanges from the six food lists each program participant is required to eat to have a healthy diet and maintain his/her ideal weight.

Activities

Facilitator	— welcomes program participants
	— passes out name tags
Group members	— share their immediate concerns
	— discuss home assignment
Facilitator	— introduces Registered Dietitian
Registered Dietitian	— lectures on healthy eating
Group members	— design a meal plan for themselves
	— make a menu for one day using the meal plan they designed
Registered Dietitian	— evaluates meal plans and menus
Facilitator	— thanks Registered Dietitian
	— summarizes session's happenings
	— gives home assignment
	— describes upcoming week's topic

Handout Materials

Meal Planning Outline
Exchange Lists for Meal Planning
Individualized Meal Plan Form
Seven Sample Menu Forms
Homework
Name Tags

Visual Aids

Meal Planning Outline Overheads
Exchange Lists for Meal Planning Overheads
Blank Overheads and Pens

Equipment

Overhead Projector
Chalkboard

References

American Diabetic Association, Inc., & The American Dietetic Association. (1986). *Exchange lists for meal planning.* Chicago: Author.

Chenault, A. A. (1984). *Nutrition and health.* New York: Holt, Rinehart and Winston.

Long, P. J., & Shannon, B. (1983). *Nutrition an inquiry into the issues.* Englewood Cliffs, NJ: Prentice-Hall.

Hamilton, E. M. N., & Whitney, E. N. (1982). *Nutrition* (2nd ed.) St. Paul, MN: West.

Whitney, E. N., & Hamilton, E. M. N. (1984). *Understanding nutrition* (3rd ed.). St. Paul, MN: West.

Meal Planning Outline

I. Establish healthy eating patterns
  A. Three nutritiously sound meals each day
  B. Appropriate number of calories to maintain weight
    1. Reducing diet
      a. Healthy diet
      b. Lose weight slowly
      c. Carefully monitored
    2. Maintenance diet weight gain
      a. Fluid retention
        1. Reduce sodium intake
          a. Reduce intake of processed food
          b. Eat more foods made from scratch
        2. Reduce salt
          a. Cooking
          b. At the table
      b. Constipation
        1. Increase fluid consumption
        2. Increase exercise
        3. Increase fiber consumption
          a. Whole grain breads and cereals
          b. Fruits and vegetables
      c. Meal plans
        1. Make in advance
        2. Follow them
II. Exchange Lists for Meal Planning
  A. Milk exchanges
  B. Vegetable exchanges
  C. Fruit exchanges
  D. Bread exchanges
  E. Meat exchanges
  F. Fat exchanges
  G. Other foods
    1. Sugar
    2. Alcohol
    3. Unlimited amounts
      a. Coffee, tea, diet pop
      b. Dill pickles, vinegar, bouillon, horseradish
      c. Herbs and spices

III. Maintenance requirements
   A. Change lbs to kg
      1. Lb wt $\times \dfrac{1 \text{ kg}}{2.2 \text{ lb}}$ = kg wt

      2. 150 lb $\times \dfrac{1 \text{ kg}}{2.2 \text{ lb}}$ = 68 kg

   B. Multiply wt in kg by BMR factor
      1. Women = .9
         a. Kg $\times \dfrac{.9 \text{ kcal}}{\text{kg per hr}}$ = kcal per hr

         b. 68 kg $\times \dfrac{.9 \text{ kcal}}{\text{kg per hr}}$ = 61 kcal per hr

      2. Men = 1
   C. Multiply kcal used in 1 hr by hrs in a day
      1. Kcal per hr $\times \dfrac{24 \text{ hr}}{1 \text{ day}}$ = kcal per day for BMR

      2. 61 kcal per hr $\times \dfrac{24 \text{ hr}}{1 \text{ day}}$ = 1464 kcal per day for BMR

   D. Activity level
      1. Sedentary = 50%
      2. Light   = 60%
      3. Moderate = 75%
      4. Strenuous = 100%
   E. Multiply the BMR kcal by activity level %
      1. Kcal per day $\times$ activity level % = kcal per day of physical activity
      2. 1464 kcal per day $\times$ .50 = 732 kcal per day of physical activity
   F. Add BMR and activity level
      1. BMR = 1464 kcal
      2. Activity level = 732 kcal
      3. Maintenance requirement = 2196 kcal

INDIVIDUALIZED MEAL PLAN FORM
FOR MAINTAINING HEALTHY EATING PATTERNS

Name_____

Date_____

Total Number of Exchanges Recommended Over the Entire Day

	Breakfast	Lunch	Snack	Dinner	Snack	Total
Milk						
Vegetable						
Fruit						
Starch/Bread						
Meat						
Fat						

SAMPLE MENU FORM

Name:_____Date:_____

	Food Item	Amount to Eat	Milk	Veg.	Fruit	Starch/ Bread	Meat	Fat
Time								
Breakfast								
Time								
Lunch								
Time								
Dinner								
	Total							
	Individualized Meal Plan							

Homework: Becoming a Healthy Eater

1. Each evening plan out in writing breakfast, lunch, dinner, and snack menus for yourself for the next day. Begin this evening. Follow this procedure for three days.
2. Each evening, evaluate in writing the ways you followed or did not follow your meal plan for the day.
3. How did your friends and family members support your healthy eating patterns? How did your friends and family members sabotage your healthy eating patterns?

Chapter IV

A TRIED AND TESTED PROGRAM

TEST SCORES

THE "Helping the Bulimic Get Better" program can help friends and family members manage problems produced by being involved with a bulimic and be supportive of their bulimic's recovery. These were the findings when the "Helping the Bulimic Get Better" program was offered three times and evaluated.

Three instruments were used to evaluate the program. They were a bulimia knowledge, bulimia attitude, and bulimia skill device (see Chapter VI). The three instruments were administered before and after concerned others attended the program. Thirty-five concerned others, who attended two or more sessions of the program, completed the pre and posttest on the skill device. Thirty-four participants, who attended two or more sessions of the program, completed the pre and posttest on the knowledge and attitude instruments. The three bulimia instruments were also administered to twenty-two significant others who did not attend the program. They were administered before and after a five-week period. A significant difference was found between the pre and posttest scores of program participants at the .05 probability level. No significant difference was found between the pre and posttest scores of significant others who did not participate in the program.

PARTICIPANTS' COMMENTS

Thirty concerned others who attended the program completed an evaluation form for the program (see Chapter VI). They rated the sessions in the program between good and excellent and the activities helpful to very helpful. Ninety-seven percent of them said they would recommend the program to others with a bulimic loved one. Reasons they gave for recommending the program included: it was "good for them"; it was "helpful"; it was "informative"; it was "a source of support"; and it "fulfilled their need to talk about being involved with a bulimic." These findings, together with the evidence that participants gained knowledge, attitudes, and skills, as a result of the "Helping the Bulimic Get Better" program, support its merit.

PRODUCING A SUCCESSFUL PROGRAM

Factors were identified which contributed to the success of the program. Offering the "Helping the Bulimic Get Better Program" for friends and relatives separate from treatment for their bulimics produced positive outcomes. Holding separate meetings for significant others provided them with the privacy they needed for considering the conflict-laden situations produced by being involved with a bulimic.

Advantages were noted for conducting the bulimia assistance program in the group setting. The group setting provided friends and family members an opportunity to identify with others experiencing common bulimia-related problems. It facilitated their ventilation of emotions and helped them feel less isolated with their bulimia produced dilemmas.

Starting the program with fifteen concerned others was determined to be beneficial. Since the ideal size for the group was eight to twelve members, beginning with fifteen members considered some participants would drop out of the program before it finished.

Scheduling meetings of the program for one and a half hours, once a week for five weeks on a Monday to Friday evening or Saturday morning was found desirable. Program participants were generally occupied with school or jobs from 8:00 a.m. to 5:00 p.m., Monday through Friday. One and a half hours was an adequate period of time to get members in the group warmed up, as well as, an appropriate length of time to maintain participants' interest in each session's topic. By meeting once a week for five weeks, it was possible to produce measurable changes in the knowledge, attitudes and behavior about bulimia of program participants and always have at least 68 percent of the participants attending each meeting.

It was useful to allow time at the beginning of each session in the program for significant others to share concerns. This freed them from thinking about their own situations, so that later when the topic of the session was introduced, they could concentrate on it, rather than on their own concerns.

The results supported using a variety of educational techniques in the program. The combination of approaches used to change program participants' knowledge, attitudes, and behavior about bulimia included lectures, movies, handouts, role-plays, overheads, discussions, case studies, and home assignments.

Scheduling information giving sessions in the first weeks of the assistance program for significant others and problem-solving sessions in later sessions worked well. Providing information during the first two sessions gave program participants time to become comfortable with one another. This enabled them to examine the more personal bulimia-related problems in the following three sessions.

In summary, these were the factors which contributed to the success of the "Helping the Bulimic Get Better" program: independent significant other meetings, a group setting, beginning with fifteen members per group, a five-week program with one-and-a-half-hour meetings, providing sharing time, using a variety of educational techniques and information sessions followed by problem-solving sessions. These findings were generally consistent with findings reported in the alcohol literature which examined programs for the significant others of alcoholics.

Chapter V

GETTING AND KEEPING PARTICIPANTS

PARTICIPANT ANONYMITY

FACTORS need to be considered which will enhance participation by friends and relatives when offering the "Helping the Bulimic Get Better" program. The information marketed about the program is one factor. For many, bulimia has negative connotations (Boskind-White & White, 1983; Kinoy et al., 1984). This may deter some concerned others from attending a bulimia assistance program. They may not be willing to publicly acknowledge their involvement with a bulimic. Informing potential participants when marketing a program that enrollment is limited to fifteen members may reduce potential participants' hesitation to register for a program. Significant others may be further encouraged to attend if they are informed individual meetings are scheduled with the program facilitator prior to the first group meeting. At this meeting they can discuss the details of the program and any concerns they have about the program privately with the program facilitator. Marketing the program to emphasize that anonymity of program participants is respected and that the site selected for the program allows meetings to be attended discretely are other techniques that may be used to enhance attendance at the program.

PARTICIPANTS' BENEFITS

The program may be made more appealing if the benefits gained by friends and family members who have attended the "Helping the Bulimic Get Better" program are noted. Attention may be called to the responses thirty friends and family members, who attended the program, gave in an anonymous evaluation of it. These were some of the things they said that may be publicized. They said, "I learned a lot"; "I know better how to be supportive"; "Found out it was ok to confront my bulimic"; "I really feel I could handle my bulimic's failure better now"; "I'm not so infused with negative feelings any longer"; and "There is so much more to know than what I thought before coming." They indicated the activities in the program, "Forced them to think about their own bulimia-related problems and how they were managing them"; "Helped them to work out ways to handle bulimia problem situations"; "Made them realize others besides themselves were struggling with being involved with a bulimic, too"; and "Provided them an opportunity to ventilate frustrations." They rated all the sessions of the program between good and excellent and the activities helpful to very helpful. When asked if they would recommend the "Helping the Bulimic Get Better" program to others with a bulimic loved one, all but one participant (97 percent) said they would.

Other benefits of the program may also be emphasized. The findings from pre and posttest scores of twenty-two concerned others who did not attend the program and thirty-four[1] concerned others who did attend the program may be highlighted. The test results showed those who attended the program became more knowledgeable about bulimia, acquired a more positive attitude towards bulimia and developed better skills in managing bulimia produced problems and supporting their bulimic's recovery. Those who did not attend the program showed no significant change in their bulimia knowledge, attitudes, or skills before and after a five-week period.

DISSEMINATING PROGRAM INFORMATION

The methods selected to share information about the program with concerned others may influence attendance at it also. One route for disseminating information about the program is through bulimics currently undergoing treatment. Boskind-White & White (1983) reported that when a bulimic acknowledges having bulimia and seeks treatment, he/she often wants his/her significant others to support his/her recovery. This can be facilitated by sending a letter to professionals or

---

1. Thirty-four program participants completed the bulimia knowledge and attitude tests. Thirty-five program participants completed the skill test.

organizations offering assistance to bulimics (see Form II). For best results each letter should be followed up with a phone call. The names of organizations working with bulimics in a given area can be determined by calling the local crisis line, hospitals, clinics, and counseling centers in the community or the American Anorexia/Bulimia Association (AABA) (201) 836-1800. The address for AABA is 133 Cedar Lane, Teaneck, NJ 07666. Treatment contacts can be expanded further by asking each of these sources for the names of other organizations or professionals providing treatment in the area.

Another route for relaying information about the program to significant others is through university and college systems. There is evidence that bulimia is very prevalent in women attending college (Squire, 1981). Information about the program can be posted on flyers around campus, shared with school counselors, health service professionals, school staff members and faculty, or publicized through a school radio station or school news publication. Form III and IV are a sample registration/flyer and a sample memo which can be sent to school professionals.

Radio and TV announcements and listings or articles in local and state newspapers are also effective channels for providing information about an assistant program for significant others to potential participants. The yellow pages of a local telephone directory can be consulted for the names and phone numbers of local radio and TV stations and local and state news publications. Then contact the radio or TV station's manager or the editor of the news publication by phone. Ask them to announce or publish information about the "Helping the Bulimic Get Better" program. Describe the public service benefits they will be providing their audiences by discussing the program. Follow up the telephone conversation with a letter including a news release or announcement. A sample of a letter to an editor, a news release, and radio announcement are provided in Form V, Form VI, and Form VII. When marketing the program in a metropolitan area, preference may be given to sharing program information with news media serving middle class neighborhoods. It appears that bulimia's victims frequently come from middle-class family backgrounds (Boskind-White & White, 1983).

Information about the program may also be shared with religious personnel. Families often turn to church pastors or other religious personnel for assistance when they are burdened by problems. Form VIII is a sample letter to a parish pastor. It is appropriate to follow the letter up with a phone call.

SCHEDULING MEETINGS

Another factor which may encourage participation in the program is arranging program meetings to coincide with the schedules of the schools in the area.

MAKING A COMMITMENT

Finally, ask concerned others to commit themselves to attending all five sessions of the "Helping the Bulimic Get Better" program. This can be done when concerned others meet individually with the program facilitator, prior to the first group meeting. Explain to friends and relatives that the number of significant others in each program offering is limited to fifteen. If several members choose not to attend a meeting, group activities may be impaired. Form I is a sample of a form that may be used to obtain concerned others' commitment to attend all the sessions of the program.

Form II

Sample Letter to Professionals

March 17, 1988

Dear Health Professional:

Beginning April 11, 12, and 13 I will be offering an assistance program for the friends and family members of women practicing or recovering from the eating disorder, bulimia. The program is described on the enclosed registration form.

I would appreciate it if you would share the information regarding this program with your bulimic clients, their significant others or anyone you feel might be interested in participating. There is no charge to attend the program. It does not matter if the concerned others are currently, or have previously, participated in some type of program/meetings for the concerned others of bulimics.

If you have any questions about the program or would like additional registration forms, please call me, ____-____.

I will be most grateful for any support you can provide in encouraging participation in this program. Thanks for your help.

Sincerely,

Sandy Kapoor,
Associate Professor

Form III

Sample Registration Form

PLEASE POST

Helping the Bulimic Get Better

Is: a program

Designed: for the relatives and friends of practicing or recovering Bulimics

To: (1) learn more about how to help their Bulimic get better
                                      and
        (2) learn to deal with the problems being involved with a Bulimic produces.

Offered: for free

In: Room 325A Vo-Tech Ed Building on the University _____ campus, 1954
        Buford Ave., _____, ____

On: 5 Thursdays, April 11 through May 9, 6:30 p.m. to 8:00 p.m.
                                      or
        5 Fridays, April 12 through May 10, 6:30 p.m. to 8:00 p.m.
                                      or
        5 Saturdays, April 13 through May 11, 10:00 a.m. to 11:30 a.m.

For More Information Contact: Sandy Kapoor

Registration Form

Name_____   Telephone (H)_____

Address_____   (W)_____

_____

When can we contact you to confirm your reservation for this program? _____
at home _____ at work _____

Please check the 5 week session you would like to register for:

_____ Thursdays April 11-May 9, 6:30 p.m. to 8:00 p.m.
_____ Fridays April 12-May 10, 6:30 p.m. to 8:00 p.m.
_____ Saturdays April 13-May 11, 10:00 a.m. to 11:30 a.m.

Mail to: Sandy Kapoor, _____, _____, _____, _____

Registration form must be received one week prior to the start of each program.

Form IV

Sample Memo to School Professionals

DATE: April 1, 1988

TO: All Faculty and Staff

FROM: Sandy Kapoor, Associate Professor

RE: Helping the Bulimic Get Better Program

It is estimated that as much as 20 percent of America's female college population suffers from the eating disorder, bulimia. Often when friends and family members discover they are involved with a bulimic, they want to help their bulimic recover, but don't know how.

Beginning April 15, a five week program will be offered for the significant others of individuals with bulimia to address this problem. There is no charge to attend the program.

I would appreciate it if you would share the attached information about this program with your students and/or any other individuals you feel might be interested in participating. If you or they have any questions about the program, please call me at ____-____.

I will be grateful for whatever support you can provide in encouraging participation in this program. Thanks for your help.

Form V

Sample Letter to Editors

March 16, 1988

Dear Editor:

I am writing to request you include the enclosed news release in the next edition of your publication. I would also like to ask you to list the information on the enclosed registration form about the friend and family bulimia assistance program, in any future editions of your publication. If you would like more information about the programs, or bulimia in general, I would be happy to provide it for you. I can be reached at ___-___.

If you do print this news release, or something about the program, could you send me a copy of it, or notify me it has been printed so I can obtain a copy. A self-addressed stamped envelope is enclosed for this purpose. I will be most appreciative of whatever you can do.

Thanks so much.

Sincerely,

Sandy Kapoor, Ph.D., M.P.H., R.D.
Associate Professor
Southwest State University

Form VI

New Release

Help the Bulimic Get Better

Binging and vomiting are often a well kept secret by women suffering from the eating disorder, bulimia. Unbelievable as it may seem, bulimics have managed to keep their behavior a total secret from family members and friends for as long as ten to fifteen years. Once the secret is disclosed those close to the bulimic often want to support their bulimic's recovery, but don't know how.

If you are the relative or friend of a practicing or recovering bulimic, a five week program will be offered to help you learn more about how to support your bulimic's recovery. The program will also help you learn how to deal with problems being involved with a bulimic produce. The program will meet five Thursdays, April 11-May 9, 6:30 p.m. to 8:00 p.m., or five Fridays, April 12-May 10, 6:30 p.m. to 8:00 p.m., or five Saturdays, April 13-May 11, 10:00 a.m. to 11:30 a.m. in 325 Vo-Tech Ed Building at the _____, _____ campus. There will be *no charge* for the program.

Register for the program by sending your name, address and phone number to:

> Sandy Kapoor
> Associate Professor
>
> _____
>
> _____, _____

For more information about the program, call Professor Kapoor at 331-3625.

Form VII

Radio Announcement

DATE: March 27, 1988

TO: Information Announcer, KMHL/KKCK Radio Station

FROM: Sandy Kapoor, Associate Professor

RE: Helping the Bulimic Get Better Program

Announcement One

A five week program for the friends and family members of women with bulimia will be offered at _____. The program will be offered Monday afternoons or evenings beginning April 15. There will be no charge for the program. For more information, call Sandy Kapoor at ___-____.

Announcement Two

It is estimated that as much as 20 percent of America's college women suffer from the eating disorder, bulimia. Often when friends and family members discover their loved one is bulimic, they want to help them get better, but don't know how. For more information on a program to help your daughter, sister, friend, or wife recover from bulimia, call Sandy Kapoor at ___-____.

Form VIII

Sample Letter to Parish Pastors

February 21, 1988

Dear Pastor:

Beginning March 11 and April 15 I will be offering an assistance program for the significant others of women practicing and recovering from the eating disorder, bulimia. The program, with the times and dates it will be offered, is described in the enclosed flyer.

I would appreciate it if you would share the information regarding this program with your parishioners via your bulletin, personal contact, or other appropriate means. If you have questions about the program, please call me _____ ___-_____.

Thank you for your help.

Sincerely,

Sandy Kapoor, Ph.D., M.P.H., R.D.
Associate Professor

SK/kf

Chapter VI

EVALUATING
A BULIMIA ASSISTANCE PROGRAM

THIS CHAPTER includes three instruments and an evaluation form. They were developed to evaluate the effectiveness of the "Helping the Bulimic Get Better" program. The instruments are a knowledge test, an attitude survey and a skill device. The three instruments and the evaluation form may be copied for evaluation purposes.

BULIMIA KNOWLEDGE TEST

Bulimia Knowledge Test was designed to measure significant others' knowledge about bulimia and healthy eating. It contains fifty multiple choice questions. They test subjects' knowledge about information presented in Session One — Understanding What Bulimia Is, Session Two — More About Bulimia and Optional Session — Becoming a Healthy eater in the "Helping the Bulimic Get Better" program.

A pilot study was conducted on the instrument. Twenty-three significant others of bulimics participated. The reliability of the instrument was calculated on the data from the pilot sample. Assessment of the internal consistency resulted in a Cronbach's alpha of .56. Internal consistency assessed by split-half reliability tests yielded a Spearman-Brown coefficient of .62 and a Guttman split-half coefficient of .62.

The pilot study data was also used to appraise the effectiveness of items in Bulimia Knowledge Test. The responses of the ten highest scoring subjects were compared with the responses of the ten lowest scoring subjects (Gronlund, 1976). Items found to be ineffective were revised to correct for poor discriminating power, ineffective distractors, unacceptable difficulty levels, and any other apparent defects.

109

The content validity of Bulimia Knowledge Test was checked while it was being developed and when it was used. It was established by preparing a table of specifications (Gronlund, 1976). Three specialists in the fields of nutrition and bulimia were also employed to evaluate the Test for content validity.

The internal consistency of Bulimia Knowledge Test was reassessed after the instrument was revised. The assessment was made on the scores of fifty-six significant others who completed the Test. It yielded a Cronbach's alpha of .73. Split-half reliability procedures produced a Spearman-Brown coefficient of .75 and a Guttman split-half coefficient of .74.

Test-retest reliability was also calculated for Bulimia Knowledge Test. The assessment was made using the scores of twenty-two significant others who completed Bulimia Knowledge Test before and after a five-week period. During this time period, they received no education about bulimia or healthy eating. The assessment yielded a Pearson product-moment correlation coefficient of .88.

The effectiveness of items in the revised form of Bulimia Knowledge Test was appraised. The appraisal was made on the scores of fifty-six friends and family members who completed the Test. Once again, Gronlund's (1976) procedure for comparing the responses of the ten highest scoring subjects with the ten lowest scoring subjects was used. The revisions to the instrument improved the discriminating power and distractor effectiveness of its items.

Bulimia Knowledge Test has the potential for assessing knowledge about bulimia and healthy eating. The instrument may be used as it is or modified to meet the needs of the program being offered. For example, if Optional Session—Becoming a Healthy Eater—is not being offered in the program, questions about healthy eating may be deleted from Bulimia Knowledge Test. They may be replaced by additional questions about bulimia or Bulimia Knowledge Test may be used with fewer questions.

BULIMIA KNOWLEDGE TEST FORM

Name_____

Date_____

Directions

There is one best answer to each question. Read each question carefully. Then circle the letter of the response you feel best answers the question. If you are unsure or don't know an answer, select the response you feel best answers the question. Before turning in your answer sheet, make sure you have marked a response for every question.

1. Bulimics are more likely to binge when they are
   a. alone
   b. with an immediate family member
   c. with a group of family members
   d. with a group of strangers
2. The disease bulimia has been found to be the most similar to is
   a. cancer
   b. depressive neurosis
   c. schizophrenia
   d. alcoholism
3. It is most acceptable for the recovering bulimic to eat
   a. the same foods for lunch every day
   b. no foods not eaten previously
   c. a variety of foods every day
   d. foods previously disliked
4. What foods are bulimics most likely to binge on?
   a. high calorie, easily ingested foods
   b. whatever foods are available
   c. no particular foods
   d. bland tasting foods
5. Diet pop is not listed in any of the exchange lists in the Exchange Lists for Meal Planning because
   a. it may promote binging
   b. it has been found to be hazardous to health
   c. it may produce fluid retention
   d. it contains insignificant amounts of calories

6. Following an eating binge, bulimics tend to feel
   a. peaceful
   b. depressed
   c. in control
   d. pleased with themselves
7. How severe the physical consequences of the bulimia are will depend most on
   a. the frequency of the binges
   b. the frequency of the purges
   c. the weight of the bulimic
   d. the age of the bulimic
8. Recovering bulimics experiencing fluid retention should reduce their intake of
   a. herbs and spices
   b. fluids
   c. meals made from box mixes
   d. raw fruits and vegetables
9. Which of the following contains two items high in fiber?
   a. popcorn, cream style corn
   b. roast chicken with the skin on, bran flakes
   c. whole wheat toast, prune juice
   d. baked beans, yogurt
10. Bulimia has been defined as a
    a. familial illness
    b. sociocultural illness
    c. psychiatric illness
    d. physical illness
11. Which meal plan below is the most acceptable for the recovering bulimic? A meal plan
    a. consisting of six small meals
    b. consisting of three small meals with one or two snacks
    c. adjusted daily according to schedule requirements
    d. established individually to account for lifestyle differences
12. Which item below should be avoided by the bulimic during the initial stages of recovery?
    a. alcohol
    b. bread
    c. red meat
    d. coffee

13. The Exchange Lists for Meal Planning allows each of the foods listed below to be eaten in unlimited amounts *except*
    a. mustard
    b. dill pickles
    c. ketchup
    d. coffee
14. In the Exchange Lists for Meal Planning, which exchange list are nuts found in?
    a. vegetable list
    b. meat list
    c. fat list
    d. varies according to type of nut
15. The most frequent age of onset for bulimia is
    a. thirteen
    b. fifteen
    c. eighteen
    d. twenty-one
16. Individuals suffering from bulimia tend to be
    a. underweight
    b. normal in weight
    c. overweight
    d. no particular weight
17. If bulimia is not treated, the bulimic will most likely
    a. attempt suicide
    b. die as a result of the physical effects
    c. become more involved in the binging and purging
    d. begin abusing alcohol
18. The reason most likely for a bulimic to terminate a binge is because they
    a. feel guilty
    b. are afraid of getting fat
    c. have abdominal pains
    d. don't have any more binge foods readily available
19. The most likely way for a bulimic to terminate a binge is by
    a. exercising
    b. having a bowel movement
    c. sleeping
    d. consuming alcohol

20. The National Association of Anorexia Nervosa and Associated Disorders estimates the percentage of college women who engage in bulimic behavior to be
    a. 5-10 percent
    b. 20-30 percent
    c. 40-50 percent
    d. greater than 50 percent
21. The most probable physical complication bulimics who purge by vomiting will have is
    a. swollen salivary glands
    b. a protruding stomach
    c. stomach cramps
    d. constipation
22. Which exchange lists does the Exchange Lists for Meal Planning place ice cream in?
    a. fat and starch/bread lists
    b. fat and milk lists
    c. starch/bread and milk lists
    d. milk and meat lists
23. How many starch/bread exchanges from the Exchange Lists for Meal Planning will a Registered Dietitian recommend most recovering bulimics eat each day?
    a. none
    b. less than four
    c. five
    d. six or more
24. The cause of bulimia is
    a. low self-esteem
    b. social emphasis on slimness
    c. stressful life situations along with no coping skills
    d. not known
25. Physically, most bulimics look
    a. healthy
    b. anemic
    c. three months pregnant
    d. frail
26. The weight gain many recovering bulimics experience initially on a weight maintenance diet is generally due to
    a. water retention
    b. the body's inability to adjust to a normal calorie intake
    c. the replacement of body tissues lost during binging and purging
    d. metabolism problems

27. In order to maintain weight, most recovering bulimics will need to eat
    a. around 1,200 calories per day
    b. 1,300 to 1,600 calories per day
    c. at least 1,800 calories per day
    d. over 3,000 calories per day
28. Menstruation in most practicing bulimics
    a. is regular
    b. is irregular
    c. ceases permanently
    d. ceases until abstinence is maintained six to twelve months
29. In the Exchange Lists for Meal Planning, exchanges from the milk exchange list may be substituted with exchanges from
    a. the starch/bread exchange list
    b. the fat exchange list
    c. any of the other exchange lists
    d. only the milk exchange list
30. Which example below from the Exchange Lists for Meal Planning contains two items from the milk exchange list?
    a. whole milk, ice cream
    b. 2 percent milk, cottage cheese
    c. yogurt, skim milk
    d. cheddar cheese, mozzarella cheese
31. The most probable effect of long term vomiting to the bulimic is
    a. reduction in stomach muscle control
    b. liver complications
    c. death
    d. irreversible tooth damage
32. When is it recommended the overweight recovering bulimic lose weight?
    a. never
    b. only when weight exceeds 25 percent of ideal weight
    c. during the initial recovery period
    d. after abstinence has been maintained for an extended period
33. Which weight pattern is a symptom used to diagnose bulimia?
    a. maintenance of weight around normal
    b. frequent weight fluctuations of more than ten pounds
    c. gradual loss of more than 20 percent of body weight
    d. maintenance of weight at levels 25 percent below normal

34. Most bulimics use this method to control their weight
    a. laxatives
    b. diuretics
    c. vomiting
    d. restrictive diets
35. Which personality description best identifies the bulimic?
    a. assertive
    b. obsessive
    c. flexible
    d. introverted
36. Which item from the meat exchange list of the Exchange Lists for Meal Planning is the highest in fat?
    a. beef tenderloin
    b. liver
    c. mozzarella cheese
    d. frankfurters
37. Bulimics experiencing constipation during the initial phase of recovery should
    a. take laxatives
    b. drink more fluids
    c. increase their consumption of starchy foods
    d. increase their consumption of dairy products
38. Which item is a vegetable exchange in the Exchange Lists for Meal Planning?
    a. lima beans
    b. corn
    c. beets
    d. green peas
39. The abbreviation used for sodium on food labels is
    a. Dp
    b. Na
    c. So
    d. Ds
40. The item below most likely to be problematic for the recovering bulimic to eat is
    a. scrambled eggs with melted cheese
    b. deep fried potato skins with sour cream
    c. toasted white bread with butter
    d. blueberry pancake with margarine and maple syrup

41. It is recommended recovering bulimics eat their meals
    a. at 8:00 a.m., 10:30 a.m., 12:00 noon, 3:00 p.m., 6:00 p.m., 8:00 p.m.
    b. as their schedule allows them each day
    c. at 8:00 a.m., 12:00 noon, 6:00 p.m.
    d. at about the same time each day
42. The major exchange lists in the Exchange Lists for Meal Planning are
    a. milk, vegetable, fruit, starch/bread, meat, fat
    b. milk, fruits and vegetables, starch/bread, meat
    c. milk, fruits and vegetables, starch/bread, meat, fat, other
    d. milk, fruit, vegetables, starch/bread, meat, miscellaneous
43. Which of the following is a symptom of bulimia?
    a. believing binge-eating is acceptable
    b. feeling binge-eating can be stopped voluntarily
    c. recurring episodes of binge-eating
    d. eating nonfood items such as dog food
44. During the initial stages of recovery, many bulimics report they
    a. experience hunger
    b. experience satiation
    c. experience both hunger and satiation
    d. experience nether hunger or satiation
45. The most effective treatment for bulimia is
    a. hospitalization
    b. drug treatment
    c. family support
    d. unknown
46. Most eating disorder specialists believe therapy for bulimia must first aim to
    a. stop the binging and purging
    b. reduce the binging and purging
    c. determine the cause of the bulimia
    d. eliminate the cause of the bulimia
47. Which of the vegetables listed below may be eaten raw in unlimited amounts by the Exchange Lists for Meal Planning?
    a. cauliflower
    b. broccoli
    c. spinach
    d. carrots

48. Which of the following is generally not included in bulimia treatment?
    a. weight reduction counseling
    b. group therapy
    c. stress management planning
    d. assertiveness training

49. Treatment for bulimia
    a. doesn't help most bulimics practicing the behavior more than 10 years at all
    b. helps only a few bulimics reduce their binging and purging
    c. helps the majority of bulimics at least reduce their binging and purging
    d. is almost 100% successful in stopping the bulimics' binging and purging

50. In the study reported by Goff, the largest number of kcals consumed by a bulimic in a binge was
    a. 1,000
    b. 5,000
    c. more than 10,000
    d. more than 30,000

ANSWER KEY FOR BULIMIA KNOWLEDGE TEST

1	a	11	b	21	a	31	d	41	d
2	d	12	a	22	a	32	d	42	a
3	c	13	c	23	d	33	b	43	c
4	a	14	c	24	d	34	c	44	d
5	d	15	c	25	a	35	b	45	d
6	b	16	b	26	a	36	d	46	a
7	b	17	c	27	c	37	b	47	c
8	c	18	c	28	b	38	c	48	a
9	a	19	c	29	d	39	b	49	c
10	c	20	b	30	c	40	d	50	c

BULIMIA ATTITUDE SURVEY

Bulimia Attitude Survey was designed to measure significant others' attitudes toward supporting a bulimic's recovery and managing the dilemmas produced by being involved with a bulimic. It presents subjects with thirty statements about bulimia. They are asked to indicate their degree of agreement with each statement by selecting a response from a five-point scale. The statements examine significant others' attitudes about five bulimia-related issues. They are significant others' attitudes about:

1. Confronting bulimic behavior.
   - Questions 9 and 17.
   - a favorable attitude is confronting bulimic behavior.
   - an unfavorable attitude is not confronting bulimic behavior.
2. Taking responsibility for the bulimic's eating disorder.
   - Questions 1, 5, 10, 14, 16, 20, 25 and 29.
   - a favorable attitude is not blaming oneself or another for the bulimic's eating disorder.
   - an unfavorable attitude is blaming oneself or another for the bulimic's eating disorder.
3. How bulimics feel about their bulimic behavior.
   - Questions 3, 8, 12, 15, 18, 23, 27 and 30.
   - a favorable attitude is bulimics find the bulimic behavior disgusting.
   - an unfavorable attitude is bulimics find the bulimic behavior acceptable.
4. What bulimics do to maintain their abstinence.
   - Questions 2, 7, 11, 22, 24, and 26.
   - a favorable attitude is it's acceptable for bulimics to make staying abstinent their first priority even if it does not consider others they are involved with.
   - an unfavorable attitude is it's not acceptable for bulimics to be inconsiderate of others regardless of what they feel will happen with their abstinence.
5. Inconveniencing themselves to support a bulimic's recovery.
   - Questions 4, 6, 13, 19, 21 and 28.
   - a favorable attitude is being willing to inconvenience oneself to support a bulimic's recovery.
   - an unfavorable attitude is not being willing to inconvenience oneself to support a bulimic's recovery.

A subject's attitude about each of these five bulimia-related factors may be reviewed independent of the subject's total score.

The reliability of Bulimia Attitude Survey was checked by several methods. Reliability tests were conducted on data collected from fifty-six significant others of bulimics. Each of them completed Bulimia Attitude Survey. Assessment of the internal consistency of the instrument resulted in a Cronbach's alpha of .83. Internal consistency was also calculated by split-half reliability tests. A Spearman-Brown coefficient of .83 and a Guttman split-half coefficient of .83 was computed.

Test-retest reliability was calculated for Bulimia Attitude Survey. It was computed on data collected on twenty-two significant others of bulimics. These subjects completed Bulimia Attitude Survey before and after a five-week period. The assessment yielded a Pearson product-moment correlation coefficient of .86.

The validity of Bulimia Attitude Survey was assessed in relation to the domain of attitudes about bulimia held by friends and relatives. Attitude statements in Bulimia Attitude Survey were compared to the attitudes described in the literature and in interviews by parties involved with bulimics. The attitude statements in Bulimia Attitude Survey were judged representative of the concerned others' attitudes about bulimia described in the literature and in the interviews.

Construct validity was also established for the instrument. Pretest and posttest scores of thirty-four concerned others were compared on Bulimia Attitude Survey. Pretest scores were obtained before concerned others participated in a five-week bulimia assistance program. Posttest scores were obtained after significant others participated in a five-week bulimia assistance program. A matched-pair t test was used. A significant difference was observed between the pretest and posttest scores of the concerned others at the .05 probability level.

Bulimia Attitude Survey has the potential for assessing attitudes about bulimia.

BULIMIA ATTITUDE SURVEY FORM

Name _____   Date _____

Directions:

This is not a test. There are no right or wrong responses to any sentences. Just answer as honestly as you can.

The sentence asks you to tell how you feel about the way bulimics and their significant others interact. Tell how you feel by blackening the appropriate letter.

Here is a practice sentence.

SA – Strongly agree
A – Agree
U – Undecided
D – Disagree
SD – Strongly disagree
SA   A   U   D   SD

Example:

One plus one equals two.   SA   A   U   D   SD

1. If a roommate knew her friend was binge eating and vomiting, but never confronted her, she is not necessarily to blame for her roommate's bulimia.   SA   A   U   D   SD

2. A recovering bulimic should accept her mother's dinner invitation, even if the bulimic feels the hot fudge pudding cake being served for dessert will make her binge.   SA   A   U   D   SD

3. Bulimics believe binging and then using laxatives or vomiting is disgusting.   SA   A   U   D   SD

4. If a recovering bulimic asks her family to dish their dinner plates in the kitchen, rather than having food on the table, they should do so.
   SA   A   U   D   SD

5. If a brother always made jokes and teased his sister about being fat, he should feel responsible for her bulimia.   SA   A   U   D   SD

6. If a recovering bulimic asks her spouse to stop eating sweets in front of her, it's okay for her spouse to say no.   SA   A   U   D   SD

7. If a recovering bulimic's five friends want to go to a smorgasbord, she should go even if she thinks it will be a problem.
   SA   A   U   D   SD

8. Bulimics wish they could stop binging and purging.
   SA   A   U   D   SD

9. If a bulimic binges after he promises his girlfriend he never will again, she should discuss it with him. SA A U D SD

10. If a husband demanded his wife to be a super mom, super wife, super career woman, her bulimia is *not* necessarily his fault.
SA A U D SD

11. It's okay for a bulimic to refuse to eat a dish a hostess has prepared just for him if he thinks it will lead to a binge.
SA A U D SD

12. When a bulimic takes money from her roommate's piggy bank to buy food for a binge, she *doesn't* feel guilty. SA A U D SD

13. If a recovering bulimic asks his mother to serve certain types of food when he is invited for dinner, it's okay for his mother to serve what she pleases. SA A U D SD

14. If a father never spent any time with his daughter while she was growing up, he should be blamed for her bulimia.
SA A U D SD

15. When a bulimic lies about eating a pan of bars her mother baked for the church bazaar, it probably *doesn't* bother her.
SA A U D SD

16. If a mother was never satisfied with her son's or daughter's achievements, she *shouldn't* be blamed for his/her bulimia.
SA A U D SD

17. If a bulimic binges after she promises her spouse she never will again, her spouse should just ignore it. SA A U D SD

18. When a bulimic eats the pizza left in the refrigerator for his brothers and sisters, he probably feels bad. SA A U D SD

19. If a recovering bulimic asks her card group to serve fruits or vegetables as a snack, they should do so. SA A U D SD

20. If a college track coach always told his athlete she could do better next time, he should feel he is the primary reason she became bulimic. SA A U D SD

21. If a recovering bulimic asks her roommates to remove the ice cream from their apartment because it's a problem for her, they should do so. SA A U D SD

22. A recovering bulimic should save leftovers even though she feels she may binge on them if they are sitting in her refrigerator.
SA A U D SD

23. When a bulimic's frequent vomiting causes the sewer to back up in her parent's home, she is probably sorry for what she has done.
SA A U D SD

24. It's okay for a recovering bulimic to tell a friend she'll bring her own food when she is invited for dinner if she thinks it will help her stay abstinent. SA A U D SD

25. If an older sister was always trying to help her younger sister go on a diet, she should feel responsible for her sister becoming bulimic. SA A U D SD

26. It's okay for a recovering bulimic to refuse to go to her in-laws home for Christmas because she feels the nonstop eating and drinking may cause her to have a binge. SA A U D SD

27. Bulimics believe vomiting or using laxatives is an acceptable way to control weight. SA A U D SD

28. If a recovering bulimic asks her college roommates to discontinue their evening popcorn parties because she is trying to recover from bulimia, it's alright if her roommates don't. SA A U D SD

29. If a boyfriend repeatedly told his girlfriend she'd look really good just ten pounds thinner, he should be blamed for her bulimia. SA A U D SD

30. When a bulimic writes a $25 bad check to buy food for a binge, she probably feels it's no big deal. SA A U D SD

ANSWER KEY FOR BULIMIA ATTITUDE SURVEY

	SA	A	U	D	SD
1.	5	4	3	2	1
2.	1	2	3	4	5
3.	5	4	3	2	1
4.	5	4	3	2	1
5.	1	2	3	4	5
6.	1	2	3	4	5
7.	1	2	3	4	5
8.	5	4	3	2	1
9.	5	4	3	2	1
10.	5	4	3	2	1
11.	5	4	3	2	1
12.	1	2	3	4	5
13.	1	2	3	4	5
14.	1	2	3	4	5
15.	1	2	3	4	5
16.	5	4	3	2	1
17.	1	2	3	4	5
18.	5	4	3	2	1
19.	5	4	3	2	1
20.	1	2	3	4	5
21.	5	4	3	2	1
22.	1	2	3	4	5
23.	5	4	3	2	1
24.	5	4	3	2	1
25.	1	2	3	4	5
26.	5	4	3	2	1
27.	1	2	3	4	5
28.	1	2	3	4	5
29.	1	2	3	4	5
30.	1	2	3	4	5

BULIMIA SKILL DEVICE

Bulimia Skill Device was developed to measure significant others' ability to support a bulimic's recovery and to manage bulimia-related problems. It presents subjects with four bulimia-produced problems. They are problems encountered by the sister, mother, husband, and friend of a bulimic. In each situation, subjects are asked how they would manage the bulimia-produced problem if they were the friend or family member faced with the problem. Subjects' responses to the four problem situations are rated with three, three-point scales. The scales evaluate subjects' ability to be supportive, to be confrontative, and to manage bulimia-related problems. Subjects' responses to each of the four problem situations may be compared before and after they attend an assistance program. This will provide further information about the effects of the program on them.

Validity was checked in the development and use of Bulimia Skill Device. It was established in relation to the domain of problems experienced by concerned others of bulimics. The problems created in the four role-play situations were compared to problem situations described in the bulimia literature and in interviews with bulimics, concerned others of bulimics and eating disorder professionals. The problems in the role-play situations were judged to be representative of concerned others' real life bulimia-related problems, as reported in the literature and in the interviews.

Construct validity was also established for Bulimia Skill Device. The pretest and posttest scores of thirty-five subjects who participated in a five-week bulimia assistance program were compared. Using a matched-pair t test, a significant difference was observed between the thirty-five subjects' pretest and posttest scores at the .05 probability level.

Reliability tests were conducted for Bulimia Skill Device. The pretest and posttest scores of thirty-five subjects who participated in a five-week bulimia assistance program were compared. Using a matched-pair t test, a significant difference was observed between the thirty-five subjects' pretest and posttest scores at the .05 probability level.

Reliability tests were conducted for Bulimia Skill Device. Test-retest reliability was assessed for the instrument. The pretest and posttest scores of twenty-two friends and relatives who did not participate in an assistance program were used. A Pearson product-moment correlation coefficient of .84 was obtained.

Interscorer agreement among four scorers was also assessed. The scorers were three college students, who had attended a three-hour educational seminar about bulimia, and the instrument developer. Each scorer was asked to score the responses of four randomly selected concerned others to the four problem situations in Bulimia Skill Device. The interscorer agreement method described by Haynes (1978) was used. The mean of the agreement coefficients calculated for the four scorers was .67. Interscorer reliability was also determined by calculating the percentage of agreement among the four scorers (Kerlinger, 1964). The mean agreement score was 80 percent.

Bulimia Skill Device has the potential for measuring significant others' skills to manage bulimia problems and support a bulimic's recovery.

BULIMIA SKILL DEVICE FORM

Equipment Needed

1. Tape recorder to record subject responses
2. Blank tape
3. Optional: tape recorder to play voices of significant others reading the problem stories
4. Optional: tape with voices of significant others telling their problem stories.

Introduction

(Narrator) This evening I'd like to do an activity with you to determine your ability to support your bulimic friend or family member's recovery from her (his) eating disorder and your ability to handle the dilemmas being involved with a bulimic are producing for you. It will involve listening to four different friends or family members describe problem situations they are faced with by being involved with a bulimic. While you are listening to each friend or family member describe their problem, I'd like you to try to imagine you are the friend or family member faced with the problem. Then you'll have the chance to verbalize what you would do if you were the friend or family member faced with the problem.

I will tape record your responses to the problem. This will make it possible for me to review them later. As you know, the contents of your tape recording will remain confidential. They will be disclosed only if you give written permission.

There are no right or wrong responses. Please respond as honestly as you can.

To help you get the swing of things, we'll go through one problem just for practice. It's a problem involving a bulimic named Mary. Each of the problems you will be asked to respond to this *(evening)* will involve Mary. They will be problems either Mary's mom, husband, sister, or friend face due to Mary's bulimia.

In our practice problem, Mary's sister, Ann, finds herself in a situation in which she doesn't know what to do. As you listen to Ann describe her problem, imagine you are Ann. Think of what you'd do if you were Ann, faced with her problem. Then you'll have a chance to tell what you'd do if you were Ann in this predicament.

Practice Story

(play tape recording of female voice telling story or narrator read story)

I'm Ann, Mary's sister. Two months ago Mary told me she was bulimic. Both Jill, our other sister, and I suspected it for a long time.

The problem is, when Mary told me she was bulimic, she asked me not to tell Jill. That was fine. But what am I supposed to do when Jill asks me if I think Mary's bulimic?

(narrator)

Imagine you are Ann. Imagine Jill has just asked you if you think Mary is bulimic. Will you describe what you'd do?

(tape record response)

(narrator)

This next problem also involves Mary's sister, Ann. Once again, Ann finds herself in a situation concerning Mary's eating disorder she doesn't know how to handle. As Ann describes her problem, again, imagine you are Ann. Then after Ann describes her predicament, you'll be able to tell what you'd do if you were Ann.

Story One

(play tape recording of female voice telling story or narrator read story)

We've already met. I'm Mary's sister, Ann. As I mentioned previously, Mary told me she was bulimic two months ago. Well today I was driving by (Haas's) Bakery. I saw Mary walk in. She didn't see me. One of Mary's favorite binge foods is cream-filled, chocolate covered long johns.

(narrator)

Imagine you are Ann. You are driving by (Haas's) Bakery and see Mary go in. What would you do?

(tape record response)

(narrator)

This time John, Mary's husband, finds himself in a situation he doesn't know how to deal with. As John describes his dilemma, imagine you are John. Think of what you would do if you were John in his situation. Then you'll be able to tell what you'd do if you really were John.

Story Two

(play tape recording of male voice telling story or narrator read story)

My name is John. My wife, Mary, and I have been married for ten years. We are both thirty now.

Before we got married, we talked a lot about having a family. We talked about our kids, what they'd be like, how many we wanted, and if we'd like boys or girls. I guess I just assumed some day I'd be a daddy.

When we were first married, Mary said she didn't want to get pregnant until we established our own relationship. Then after that, she didn't want to get pregnant because of her job. She's had a new excuse every year for why she shouldn't get pregnant, just yet. Now I know the real reason. She's bulimic.

(narrator)

What would you do if you were John? Mary has just told you the real reason she won't get pregnant is because she's bulimic. She doesn't think she can have a healthy baby.

(tape record response)

(narrator)

This next problem is one faced by Mary's mom. She finds herself in a situation with Mary she doesn't know how to deal with. We'll follow the same procedures as in our previous situations. Only this time, imagine you are Mary's mom.

Story Three

(play tape recording of female voice telling story or narrator read story)

I'm Mary's mom. A few months ago Mary told me she was bulimic. She hasn't binged or vomited since then.

Mary is visiting her Dad and me for a few days now. She comes every summer when her husband, John, goes fishing with the guys.

Last night was her first night here. About midnight I woke up. I heard someone in the kitchen. I laid in bed for the longest time, just listening. Then I got up very quietly and tiptoed to the kitchen. I just peeped my head in the door. Mary was sitting at the table. In front of her was a mixing bowl filled with ice cream, all covered with chocolate sauce. She was so busy eating, she didn't even see me.

(narrator)

Imagine you are Mary's mom. Imagine you have just found Mary in the middle of the ice cream binge. What would you do?

(tape record response)

(narrator)

This is our final dilemma. This time Mary's friend, Deb, finds herself in a predicament involving Mary she doesn't know how to deal with. As Deb describes her problem, imagine you are Deb. Then you'll have a chance to tell what you'd do if you were Deb in her predicament.

Story Four

(play tape recording of female voice telling story or narrator read story)

My name is Deb. I'm Mary's friend. Mary and I have been close friends since we were kids. A few months ago Mary told me she was bulimic. We haven't seen each other since then.

So today we made plans to go to the annual community, luncheon fashion show. It's this coming Saturday. I offered to pick up the tickets. Mary's going to pay me on Saturday. Tickets are $40. That's expensive for both of us. But we agreed. We deserved to treat ourselves. What the heck!

After I bought the tickets I decided to give Mary a call, just to let her know everything was set. I told her how much fun it was going to be and that I could hardly wait. I'd gotten us really good seats. After all this, she said she hated to do this to me, but would I mind if she cancelled out on Saturday. She just didn't think, with her bulimia, she could handle the five course luncheon that would be served while the fashion show was going on.

(narrator)

Imagine you are Deb. Mary has just told you she doesn't want to go to the fashion show on Saturday. What would you do?

(tape record response)

ANSWER KEY FOR BULIMIA SKILL DEVICE

Introduction

Significant others of a bulimic were asked to listen to four stories about problems faced by the sister, husband, mom, and friend of a bulimic, named Mary. They were then requested to verbalize how they would handle each problem situation, if they were that person.

Directions

Please read each problem situation carefully. Then read the subject's response to each problem story. Finally, score the subject's response to each problem story on the attached score sheet. Scoring information for the device follows. In the event that a subject is not sure what they would do in a particular situation, and responds in more than one way, use the response they give first for scoring purposes.

Bakery (Sister) Situation

Score

Confrontation

3 = Confronted Immediately
2 = Confronted at a Later Time
1 = Did not Confront

Support

3 = Very Supportive
2 = Somewhat Supportive
1 = Not Supportive

Pregnant (Husband) Situation

Score

Managed Dilemma

3 = Managed Own Dilemma Very Well
2 = Managed Own Dilemma Somewhat
1 = Managed Own Dilemma Poorly

Support

3 = Very Supportive
2 = Somewhat Supportive
1 = Not Supportive

Ice Cream (Mom) Situation

Score

Confrontation

3 = Confronted Immediately
2 = Confronted at a Later Time
1 = Did not Confront

Support

3 = Very Supportive
2 = Somewhat Supportive
1 = Not Supportive

Fashion Show (Friend) Situation

Score

Managed Dilemma

3 = Managed Own Dilemma Very Well
2 = Managed Own Dilemma Somewhat
1 = Managed Own Dilemma Poorly

Support

3 = Very Supportive
2 = Somewhat Supportive
1 = Not Supportive

Descriptions of Behavior Revealing Confrontation, Support and Dilemma Management at Levels 3, 2, and 1

Bakery (Sister) Situation

Confrontation

Confronted Immediately = 3.

Ann - went into the bakery and verbally or by mere presence acknowledged to Mary that the bakery may be a problem for Mary

Confronted at a Later Time = 2.

Ann - addressed the bakery situation with Mary at some point in time after she left the bakery

Did Not Confront = 1.

Ann - did not address the bakery situation at any point in time with Mary
     - did not reveal whether she would confront Mary

Support

Very Supportive = 3.

Ann - took action to prevent the bakery situation from being a slip
     - explored alternative plans of action to resolve the bakery problem
     - explored alternative plans of action which could be implemented to avoid similar situations presenting problems in the future
     - implemented a plan of action with Mary to satisfactorily resolve the bakery problem
     - told Mary that she stopped because she knew the bakery might be a problem
     - expressed disapproval, along with assistance in managing the problem satisfactorily
     - stayed in the bakery with Mary as support

Somewhat Supportive = 2.

Ann - offered some support, but could have offered more
     - said would help, but didn't say how
     - opened self up so Mary could ask for help
     - told Mary the importance of getting help

- offered to help Mary at the bakery or later
- asked how could be supportive at the bakery or later
- indicated disapproval with minimal assistance in managing the problem satisfactorily
- walked in and out of the bakery

Not Supportive = 1.

Ann - offered no help at the bakery or later, regarding the bakery problem, or similar future problems which might occur
- did nothing to prevent a potential slip
- talked with Mary, but since she didn't indicate what she said it may not have been supportive
- did not reveal if she would offer Mary support at the bakery or later
- did not address Mary's bulimia
- challenged Mary to buy the rolls
- suggested Mary binge or purge
- allowed Mary to binge or purge in presence
- told Mary after the bakery scene had passed she shouldn't do that

Pregnant (Husband) Situation

Managed Dilemma

Managed Own Dilemma Very Well = 3.

John - took action to resolve the problem, i.e., told Mary she must get help
- accepted Mary's news feeling it produced no problems for himself
- considered Mary's problem of primary importance now and would discuss a family later
- would try to find out more about bulimia and its affects on having a baby
- indicated would seek outside help alone or with Mary
- discussed the impact of Mary's news on self along with what needed to be done to resolve the problem now
- discussed what Mary must do about her bulimia so children would be possible
- indicated disappointment in Mary and went on to discuss how the problem could be handled

Managed Own Dilemma Somewhat = 2.

John – encouraged Mary to get help
      – resolved the problem somewhat
      – indicated what he would like to happen to resolve the problem
      – indicated to Mary his disappointment, but did not discuss how the situation could be changed for the better
      – discussed with Mary the impact of her problem on himself, but made no attempt to address resolving the problem

Managed Own Dilemma Poorly = 1.

John – was not prepared to do anything to resolve the dilemma
      – refused to discuss the problem
      – would not accept the predicament
      – did not want to hear about the problem
      – blamed himself for the problem
      – did not address the effects of Mary's problem on himself
      – ended the relationship

Support

Very Supportive = 3.

John – assisted Mary in getting help for her bulimia
      – took action to help Mary recover
      – offered to attend treatment with Mary for her bulimia
      – indicated he didn't know enough about bulimia to do anything, but would take action to learn

Somewhat Supportive = 2.

John – offered some support but could have offered more
      – offered help
      – asked how he could support Mary's recovery from bulimia
      – encouraged Mary to get help for her bulimia
      – indicated disapproval of the bulimia with minimal assistance in managing the problem
      – insisted Mary get help, but didn't assist her in getting it
      – asked how he could support Mary's recovery from bulimia
      – discussed treatment for the bulimia
      – expressed joy that Mary had shared her problem with him

Not Supportive = 1.

John – offered no help
>   – told Mary it was her problem
>   – indicated he didn't care
>   – refused to talk about the bulimia
>   – did not address the bulimia
>   – did not reveal he would offer Mary support in recovering from her bulimia
>   – talked with Mary, but since he didn't indicate what he said, it could have been something that deterred her recovery

Ice Cream (Mom) Situation

Confrontation

Confronted Immediately = 3.

Mom – went into the kitchen and acknowledged the binge to Mary

Confronted at a Later Time = 2.

Mom – acknowledged the binge at some point after it was finished, to Mary

Did Not Confront = 1.

Mom – never acknowledged the ice cream binge to Mary
>   – did not reveal whether she would confront Mary

Support

Very Supportive = 3.

Mom – helped Mary make her own action plan to deal with her problem
>   – took action to stop the behavior
>   – took action to help Mary return to recovery
>   – discussed what caused the slip and/or how it might be prevented from happening again
>   – expressed disapproval, along with assistance in managing the problem satisfactorily
>   – discussed with Mary how the problem could be resolved

Somewhat Supportive = 2.

Mom – offered some support, but could have offered more
>   – said would help, but didn't say how
>   – encouraged Mary to get help

- discussed Mary's problem without seeking methods to re-solve it
- offered help
- let Mary talk about her problem
- indicated disapproval with minimal assistance in managing the problem satisfactorily
- opened herself up so Mary could ask for help

Not Supportive = 1.

Mom – challenged Mary to continue in the binge-purge cycle
- offered no help that night or later, regarding the ice cream problem, or with similar future problems which might occur
- never acknowledged the ice cream problem
- talked with Mary, but since she didn't indicate what she said, it may not have been supportive
- did not reveal if she would offer Mary support in her eating problem

Fashion Show (Friend) Situation

Managed Dilemma

Managed Own Dilemma Very Well = 3.

Deb – told Mary she thought she should go
- accepted the cancellation feeling it was no problem
- indicated disappointment with Mary's decision to cancel the date and discussed how it could be prevented from happening again
- discussed the impact of Mary's decision on herself and/or how the problem could be resolved to her own satisfaction
- discussed how future engagements with Mary should be handled to avoid last minute cancellations

Managed Own Dilemma Somewhat = 2.

Deb – accepted Mary's decision somewhat
- indicated to Mary her disappointment, but did not discuss how this situation could be prevented from happening again
- discussed with Mary the impact of Mary's decision on herself, but did not discuss with Mary how the problem could be resolved
- resolved the problem somewhat

Managed Own Dilemma Unsatisfactorily = 1.

Deb – did not reveal to Mary feelings regarding her date cancellation
   – considered Mary to no longer be a friend
   – refused to discuss the problem
   – did not address the effect of Mary's problem on herself

Support

Very Supportive = 3.

Deb – explored how the five-course lunch could be handled so going to the fashion show would be possible
   – accepted Mary's decision and discussed doing an activity other than the fashion show now or later
   – discussed with Mary how she could resolve her problem
   – reinforced Mary for staying abstinent

Somewhat Supportive = 2.

Deb – asked how she could be supportive of Mary's recovery
   – discussed Mary's problem without seeking methods to solve it

Not Supportive = 1.

Deb – insisted Mary go to the fashion show and luncheon against her will
   – tried to persuade Mary to go without resolving the food issue
   – insisted Mary attend the fashion show without planning how the five-course lunch would be managed
   – did not address Mary's problem with her
   – did not offer Mary help in managing the eating problem
   – agreed to handle the situation as Mary requested, after trying to guilt her into going
   – indicated disapproval of Mary's decision, but accepted it
   – talked with Mary, but since she didn't indicate what she said it may not have been supportive

SCORE SHEET FOR BULIMIA SKILL DEVICE

SITUATION   SKILL

	Confrontation	*Support*	*Managed Dilemma*
Bakery (Sister) Situation	————	————	
Pregnant (Husband) Situation		————	————
Ice Cream (Mom) Situation	————	————	
Fashion Show (Friend) Situation		————	————
Total Score ———— (Sum of confrontation, support and managed dilemma scores)	———— (Total)	———— (Total)	———— (Total)

Maximum Score = 24 points
Confrontation = 6 points
Support = 12 points
Managed dilemma = 6 points

PARTICIPANT EVALUATION

The Evaluation Form was developed to obtain an anonymous, independent evaluation of the "Helping the Bulimic Get Better" program by its participants. The Form rates each session of the program and the primary activities used in the program. It may be modified to evaluate an assistance program covering topics and using activities different from those listed on this form.

EVALUATION FORM

Helping the Bulimic Get Better Program

Rate Each Session:	Excellent	Good	Fair	Poor
Session One: Understanding What Bulimia Is Explain: _____	_____	____	____	____
Session Two: More About Bulimia Explain: _____	_____	____	____	____
Session Three: Coping with Food Situations Involving the Bulimic Explain: _____	_____	____	____	____
Session Four: Dealing with the Bulimic's Failure to be Abstinent Explain: _____	_____	____	____	____
Session Five: Helping the Bulimic be Abstinent Explain: _____	_____	____	____	____

Rate the Activities:	Very Helpful	Helpful	Somewhat Helpful	Not Very Helpful
Home Assignments Explain: _____	_____	_____	_____	_____
Role-Play Activities Explain: _____	_____	_____	_____	_____

Rate the Activities (Continued):	Very Helpful	Helpful	Somewhat Helpful	Not Very Helpful
Discussions with Group Members	_____	_____	_____	_____

Explain: _____

_____

_____

_____

Would you recommend this program to others with a bulimic loved one? ____ yes ____ no

Explain: _____

_____

_____

_____

Would you be interested in participating in further sessions of this program addressing issues like forgiving, removing blame, and releasing responsibility? ____ yes ____ no

Explain: include topics you would like to see addressed in future sessions. _____

_____

_____

_____

REFERENCES

American Psychiatric Association. (1980). *Diagnostic and statistical manual of mental disorders* (3rd ed.). Washington, D.C.: Author.

Boskind-White, M., & White, W.C., Jr. (1983). *Bulimarexia the binge/purge cycle*. New York: W. W. Norton.

Cauwels, J. M. (1983). *Bulimia the binge-purge compulsion*. New York: Doubleday.

Cork, R.M. (1956). Casework in a group setting with wives of alcoholics. *Social Worker, 24,* (3), 1-6.

Gliedman, L.H., Rosenthal, D., Frank, J.D., & Nash, H.T. (1956). Group therapy of alcoholics with concurrent group meetings of their wives. *Quarterly Journal of Studies on Alcohol, 17,* 655-670.

Goff, G.M. (1984). *Bulimia: The binge-eating and purging syndrome*. Center City, MN: Hazelden.

Gronlund, N.E. (1976). *Measurement and evaluation in teaching* (4th ed.). New York: MacMillan.

Halmi, K.A., Falk, J.R., & Schwartz, E. (1981). Binge-eating and vomiting: A survey of a college population. *Psychological Medicine, 11,* 697-706.

Hatsukami, D., Owen, P., Pyle, R., & Mitchell, J. (1982). Similarities and differences of the MMPI between women with bulimia and women with alcohol or drug abuse problems. *Addictive Behaviors, 7,* 435-439.

Haynes, S.W. (1978). *Principles of behavioral assessment*. New York: Gardner Press.

Igersheimer, W.W. (1959). Group psychotherapy for nonalcoholic wives of alcoholics. *Quarterly Journal of Studies on Alcohol, 20,* 77-85.

Johnson, D., & Berndt, D.J. (1983). Preliminary investigation of bulimia and life adjustment. *American Journal of Psychiatry, 140* (6), 774-777.

Joyce, B., & Weil, M. (1978). *Personal models of teaching*. Englewood Cliffs, NJ: Prentice-Hall.

Kapoor, S. A. (1986). Effects of an educational intervention on the significant others of bulimics (Doctoral dissertation, University of Minnesota, 1986). *Dissertation Abstracts International, 47,* 2958A.

Kerlinger, F.W. (1964). *Foundations of behavioral research*. New York: Holt, Rhinehart and Winston.

Kinoy, B.P., Miller, E.B., Atchley, J.A., & Book Committee of the American Anorexia/Bulimia/Association. (1984). *When will we laugh again?* New York: Columbia University Press.

McDowell, F.K. (1972). The pastor's natural ally against alcoholism. *Journal of Pastoral Care, 26,* 26-32.

Neuman, P.A., & Halvorson, P.A. (1983). *Anorexia nervosa and bulimia.* New York: Van Nostrand-Reinhold.

Shaftel, F.R., & Shaftel, G. (1976). *Role-playing for social values: Decision making in the social studies.* Englewood Cliffs, NJ: Prentice-Hall.

Shaftel, F.R., & Shaftel, G. (1982). *Role-playing in the curriculum* (2nd ed.). Englewood Cliffs, NJ: Prentice-Hall.

Smith, C.G. (1969). Alcoholics; their treatment and their wives. *British Journal of Psychiatry, 115,* 1039-1042.

Sprinthall, R.C., & Sprinthall, N.A. (1981). *Educational psychology: A developmental approach* (3rd ed.). Reading, MA: Addison-Wesley.

Squire, S. (1981, October). Why thousands of women don't know how to eat normally anymore. *Glamour,* pp. 245, 309-311.

Stangler, R.S., & Printz, A.M. (1980). DSM-III: Psychiatric diagnosis in a university population. *American Journal of Psychiatry, 137,* 937-940.

INDEX

147